The Demon in Disguise:
Murder, Kidnapping, and the Banty Rooster

by Ashley Elliot with Michael J. Coffino

ISBN 978-1-64663-430-9

REVIEW COPY: This is an advanced printing subject to corrections and revisions.

Published by

 köehlerbooks™

3705 Shore Drive
Virginia Beach, VA 23455
800-435-4811
www.koehlerbooks.com

THE
DEMON
IN
DISGUISE

MURDER, KIDNAPPING, AND THE BANTY ROOSTER

A TRUE CRIME STORY

ASHLEY ELLIOTT
WITH MICHAEL J. COFFINO

VIRGINIA BEACH
CAPE CHARLES

TO MY DADDY

You once told me, the "truth will set me free," and it has indeed.
I DID NOT GIVE UP, LET UP, OR SHUT UP. I GAVE IT MY ALL
DESPITE THE HIGH PRICE I PAID ALONG THE WAY.

TO MY CHILDREN

This is a testimony to my God, His timing, His promises,
and His justice. Never forget that this is a small glimpse of my life
and by no means defines our family. Despite our shortcomings,
we are without a shadow of a doubt an incredible family.
I love you both.

TABLE OF CONTENTS

COMMENTS ON SOURCE MATERIAL

THIS BOOK IS BASED ON actual events and presented to the best of my knowledge.

We used many sources to create content, including third-party interviews, investigative and court files, media publications and programs, online research, and a smattering of written materials I had created or collected before undertaking this project.

This book also relies in part on my memory and personal interpretation of certain events. In a few cases, as the context will show, I share imagination, assumptions, and opinions.

Conversations and commentary are set forth as accurately as I can recall them. In some cases, conversations were reconstructed and reflect the substance of what was said as best I recall.

The specific descriptions of what occurred in courtrooms are based on available court records and interviews, and to a much lesser extent, my memory. Trial testimony and colloquy are pulled from trial transcripts and are verbatim representations, except where we cleaned up language and summarized proceedings for ease of reading and narrative flow.

Even though most of the events described in this book are in the public domain, I changed many names and identifying details to maintain anonymity.

This book is about what happened to my world when my father was murdered and mother kidnapped. It is told from the singular perspective of my pain and trauma. I am mindful others might have experienced the described events through a different lens. The story that follows is my personal rendition of what it was like to be a crime victim. It is my story and my story alone.

PREFACE

THERE WILL BE PEOPLE WHO won't be happy I have written this book.

Some will say what's done is done. The criminal justice system ran its course, straight to the hallowed courtroom of the Arkansas Supreme Court. Move on, girl.

Others won't want the dirty laundry of yesteryear aired. Let bygones be bygones.

Some family members may roll their eyes and lament—there I go again, stirring up shit, reminiscent of my wilder days. Time to grow up.

I've heard it all before. When I pressed prosecutors to do their job, people told me, "you need to let this go." I was warned I risked unleashing a hornets' nest best left undisturbed and less harmful.

I paid them little or no heed. I wanted the justice system to do what it was set up to do.

Unlike others, I didn't have the luxury of bolting the doors of the past and locking away what happened. I couldn't proceed merrily ahead, despite the passage of what many, I am sure, think was ample time to move on.

The past remains my present.

Forgetting isn't something I can do or, frankly, want to do, at least not yet. Telling my story and reliving the details are as important to me as my next breath.

I wrote this book not so much to provide an exposé of the criminal justice system, although that will follow naturally enough, but to come to better terms with what happened one grisly late Saturday night in a small Arkansas town many years ago. I had to know more and sift through the details of events that shattered my world. I had to know more because those ghastly crimes ripped apart what was left of my family and cast a dark shadow over my life. I had to know because, who wouldn't want to know what brought about such horrors? Isn't that the natural thing to do?

I didn't know what to expect when I set out to write this book. I assumed it might bring some closure. I also knew it was a gamble. It could send me into darker places, make life more difficult, and complicate things for my husband and children.

As it turned out, it has allowed me to come to grips with who I was before what happened, who I became after, and who I can be despite it all. For that much, I am grateful.

I know I can't make the scars disappear, no matter how much work I put in. The wounds are too deep. Nor am I inclined to forgive and become magically purified of pain. Forgiveness can wait its turn in the long line of healing.

I also don't see myself as a victim. That is important for me to say. I am, for lack of a better term, a survivor. I didn't dodge the awfulness of it. I faced the ugliness head on. I didn't feel sorry for myself then and I don't feel sorry now.

Playing the victim would put me in the sad place of excuse-making to explain my failings, shortcomings, and errant behavior. I don't want any of that, never did. I am not interested in pity. I don't want people uncomfortable in my presence because of what happened. I don't want people staring at me in the distance, having whisper-filled sidebars about that "poor thing." I want a wide berth of passage, without emotional crutches, to live my life the way I am destined to live it, free of sympathy. I think that is fair.

I have learned a simple fact: life goes on with or without you. Time has neither a pause nor off button. It ticks away mindlessly and unapologetically, and you either get on the bus or you don't, no matter how rocky the ride or tortuous the path. I am okay with that. That's how it is for all of us, it seems. No special treatment, please.

This book inevitably filled in many blanks in what happened one immeasurably sad weekend in 2002, an excavation of truth that had confounded some in law enforcement for a substantial period. As much as I learned back then, the past year has opened me to much more about what led to the events that are chronicled in this book.

Still, I know I don't have the entire truth, and likely never will. Among the lies, refusals to fess up, people taking last breaths armed with undisclosed information, and prosecutorial complacency, various parts of the story have gaps that cannot be filled, at least not by me. That is how it must be.

I drilled down as far as I reasonably could. I received some help along the way, as recounted in the acknowledgments, and for that I am most grateful. But I also hit dead ends with some people who now, many years afterward, don't want to get involved. I wish they had been more charitable, but I understand their reluctance. This is not their battle. It is mine alone. I also got treated, with some refreshing exceptions, to bureaucratic jerk-arounds by certain government agencies who responded to public records requests with lengthy excuse-filled form letters, but without that free information the legislation commands be doled out.

The journey of this book has been an emotional whirlwind. I still have days when I can't believe what happened, and others when I can push the sordid events of the past off the center stage of my psyche. Sometimes memories cast darkness on my spirit. Other times they demand more of me, like an acute pain in the gut. I still cry. I still get angry. I still resent certain people. I assume those feelings will continue. For how long? Perhaps forever.

Each day, however, I take another step in the right direction, making the climb up the steep incline more firmly, like stubbornly navigating a difficult hiking trail. Progress in tiny increments can be powerful—and assuring.

A new normal is taking hold, and for that, I have mainly my husband and children to thank—and my therapist.

This is my story as best as I can tell it.

PART I

1

May 19, 2002, 6:45 PM
Conway, Arkansas

"9-1-1."

"Yeah, we have an emergency in Shady Valley."

"What's the problem?"

"There's some people shot next door."

"Next door where?"

"Shady Valley, 4 Shady Valley. Next door to 4 Shady Valley. I don't know what the situation is, but some girl just came over, running to my house like crazy . . . . She said everybody had been shot in that house."

"Everybody been shot in the house?"

"Yeah."

"What is the address for that house?"

"I'm 4, so it might be 6 . . . ."

"Okay . . . units, be advised, I have received a call from number 4 Shady Valley, number 4 Shady Valley. Subject, Mr. Jake Wiles, stated that a girl came over from next door and said everyone in the residence next door had been shot. Any units available for response, please indicate."

"This is 220. Fire and EMTs are en route."

"Go ahead and notify the coroner."

"10-4."

"Tried to call Sergeant Barrett. I didn't get him on his cell phone, and his home phone is busy. Would you call and break that line and tell him what's going on?"

"We have found Sergeant Barrett. He's on his way."

"10-4."

In 2002, a 9-1-1 call about a multiple homicide, as one investigator would later put it "wasn't your run-of-the-mill crime in Conway." The news instantly swelled, as a prosecutor described, into "a black cloud that hung over the city of Conway . . . that needed to be lifted."

That is not to say that Conway, Arkansas was a backwater town. At the time it boasted a population of some 40,000 and was the seat of Faulkner County and home to three universities. Its origins as a railroad town positioned it to blossom into a major economic and cultural Arkansas hub.

Still, it was close knit.

Conway is the Taco Bell drive-thru after midnight on a Friday night. Conway is playing cards for money, with modest limits, at the local Supper Club. Conway is hardworking families, conservative values, and country music. Conway is church attendance on Sunday with hangovers from a late Saturday night rendezvous in Little Rock. Conway is thriving local businesses, people having your back, community barbecues, and genuinely warm smiles for strangers. Conway is, you stay local forever.

Conway is not a font of homicide.

Conway did lack the country charm of our prior home in Greenbriar, Arkansas, once my safe haven. Greenbriar had one four-way stop, a drug store, and a few other things, but mostly it had the best times of my life.

From the adult perspective, Conway was doubtless an upgrade from Greenbriar. My parents, Carter and Lark Elliott, moved our family of four—my older brother Trey being the other member—from Greenbriar to Conway to give our standard of living a shot in the arm and put my father closer to the bustling business he had founded in Conway at Detco Industries.

The move from Greenbriar followed relatively brief family stints in Houston, Texas and El Dorado, Arkansas, which really are a blur except for a relentless religious indoctrination courtesy of the Assembly of God faith ("all other religions are wrong")—a weekly diet of clapping and raising of the hands, speaking in tongues, and getting slain in the spirit. Toe the faithful line, children, lest you wind up on an express train to hell, pious code for no drinking, smoking, sex, music, and foul language. Yeah, that worked out fine.

Conway became the decisive attempt to cast our long-term anchor. We had a bigger home, located in the Shady Valley subdivision, a neighborhood whose residents tended toward affluent. Shady Valley bordered the Conway Country Club, literal walking distance. We weren't rich, at least I didn't think so, but my parents found a way to claim a perch among the upper echelon. Except we didn't socialize with them. We gravitated to our church community and the families of my father's business associates.

We were a traditional family by standard measures.

My father was the breadwinner and absent most of the time, working hard and often. He seemed an intensely driven man.

My mom did whatever else was needed. She made us breakfast, packed lunches for my brother and me every day, made homemade dinners, and baked cookies regularly and homemade birthday cakes. She was our protective universe, perfect in my eyes, capable of handling anything thrown her way. She hung the moon and the stars, and she was drop-dead gorgeous.

We were living our version of a Norman Rockwell painting. To the casual observer, we had it all—wholesome God-fearing southerners living a comfortable, spirited, and blessed life.

The inside showcased an entirely different reality. It was a tumultuous environment where time bombs regularly threatened to—and often did—go off. The life we had was a far cry from what I considered normal. Sure, like most families, we had our share of routines and customs, punctuated by the occasional sweet moment. But at the core we were horribly dysfunctional.

As a young girl, I hoped against hope that somehow, some way, we'd find our way out of the madness and we'd become normal, that we might return to the idyllic periods of our origins, meaning our Greenbriar farm life with horses, garden variety farm animals, and warm breezes across the front porch.

It was not in the cards. We were on a collision course. There'd be no escaping ourselves.

At some point, my parents began to argue often. I could never tell what about or whether the spats had anything to do with Trey and me. I assumed at first that is what adults do, part of the job description. Argue and make up, and return dutifully to routines.

Then, the tiffs became more frequent and louder, and a pattern developed. My father would lay into my mother in a mean way, making her cry. He never put his hand on her that I ever saw, but the intensity unsettled me, and was at times frightening, especially when an argument lasted days, as many did.

The home atmosphere became an emotional tinderbox, depending on my father's mood. If he had a good day, we'd be back to Norman Rockwell. He'd come home and lie on the couch or in his chair and kick back. I sometimes would join him, sit in his lap, or take off his shoes and rub his feet. I cherished hanging out with him. I delighted in being Daddy's little girl.

If, however, he came home irritated about something, then sound the alarm and find cover, for the shit was about to hit the fan.

Our home ebbed and flowed with his temperament *du jour*.

My father didn't drink much in those days that I knew. He had a short fuse and low tolerance for most things that didn't align with what he expected and demanded. He wasn't terribly accommodating or understanding. He didn't communicate as much as instructed.

The fighting didn't always escalate beyond the initial shouting match. It could be a one-off, like having a single round of pugilism to let off steam and calling it a day. In those cases, the storm would pass, and family routines resumed. When it got super-heated, though, my father had this ugly habit of taking the car keys from my mother, as well as her wallet and driver's license, a power play to control her and keep us stranded at home, while he did what he wanted.

My father's frustrations didn't include us kids at first. But as we got older and started to act out, when we disobeyed the rules and ruffled the feathers, things changed. My brother increasingly became the object of my father's rage. As Trey grew into a typical teenager, he pushed limits with greater frequency. For minor transgressions, family misdemeanors, Trey got treated to an old-fashioned tongue lashing and often exile to his room. For major offenses, however, family felonies, his increasingly more commonplace violations, Trey got a serious southern spanking.

I often wondered how humiliating it must have been, getting spanked in front of your little sister. My father was horribly mean to Trey in those days, which I guess explains in part why Trey, growing up, was horribly mean to me. But for whatever reason, I escaped the corporal punishment Trey received. Daddy's little girl status had its advantages.

Between the normal yelling and Trey's regular battery of punishments, the once intermittent home tension became the status quo. I became more anxious. I worried about what might happen. I paid closer attention to the mood swings around me, trying to anticipate the next grenade toss. I wanted to defend my mom and brother whenever my father laid into them. I wanted to become a protector, even tried it—once.

I was up late listening to one of my parents' raucous battles. I became concerned that my father was hitting my mother. I jumped out of bed, left my room, and flung open their bedroom door. There I stood, in the door jamb, a tiny valiant warrior, dressed to defend in pink PJs, and demanded he stop whatever he was doing. My father barked at me, in a thundering voice that blew a rush of hostile air into my face, "You need to leave the room now!" Beaten down, I hung my head and skulked away, dragging my pride back to my room.

I remained a spectator to craziness. I suppose I should have been grateful that the worst for me was a front row seat. But in hindsight, I wish I had stepped up more, been the mouse that roared. It probably would have gotten me spanked, and it wouldn't have altered the course of the sad events that later unfolded. But at least I would have taken a stand.

We had morphed from a small-town life on a farm in Greenbrier to a combustible life behind closed doors in shitty Shady Valley.

Then darker shadows prowled.

One night while I tried to sleep in my bedroom, my parents launched one of their vintage altercations. I couldn't make out their words, but the voices were raised more than normal. I assumed the brawl was about money, their favorite debate topic. My father like to make money and give it away, to the church, random people, or the charity case of the day. My mother, while not an obscene spender, enjoyed nice things. My father's impulses and control over the money often clashed with Mom's simple requests.

The voices lowered to quiet. I heard footsteps getting near. The door to my bedroom flung open and an agitated Mom strutted in. She was fully clothed, as if about to sit down to dinner. I leaned up in bed and beamed bewilderment.

"I'm sleeping in your bed tonight," she said, adding, "and so you know, I've got a gun."

You have a what? Are you fucking kidding me?

I was stunned silent. I had never seen a gun and didn't know we had one in the house.

"Mom, what's going on?" I eked out.

She slipped into my bed, fully clothed and armed with a weapon, got snugly under the covers, and eased into sleep. Conversation over. It was bedtime.

For the first time, I had palpable fear. I feared for my mother. I feared for Trey. I feared for myself.

I feared my father.

It is one thing to spank your kids. I got that part, didn't like it, but understood its place in the spectrum of southern discipline. But needing a gun to protect yourself from your husband or father was an entirely different cosmos of concern.

I began to have freaky thoughts. What the fuck is Dad going to do to us? What the fuck is Dad going to do to Mom? What might Mom do to Dad? What might Dad do to himself?

I wasn't prepared for what came next.

2

DURING A TRIP TO VISIT the family of my mother's sister, Gaye Clark and her husband Kevin Clark in Bountiful, Utah, we stopped in Price, Utah, to allow my mom me to go to the bathroom. After we did our business and freshened up, my mother retrieved a penny from her pocket and placed it delicately on top of the toilet lid, and said, "Ashley, I'm divorcing your father."

The penny ritual was a new one, but I can't say the announcement shocked me. I felt relief. Perhaps a divorce would end the fighting. The Lark and Carter Show might get cancelled, setting us free from my father's endless control.

Not long after the grand placing of the penny, a police squad car showed up at the house. My mom had evidently obtained some sort of court order. My grandparents on my mother's side had come from El Dorado, three hours away, to support my mother. My father was on his way home after picking up Trey at school. I asked my mom for clarity, and all I got was, "Everything's okay, everything will be fine." Whatever you say, Mom.

When moments later my dad arrived, the cop joined us and my father packed a bunch of things. He was getting summarily kicked out of his home. But what knocked my socks off, what sent me for a loop, was that Trey was going too. What was up with that? My father and brother were moving out as a team, with no game plan or information? All I knew was that Mom and I were about to go it alone.

I was reminded of a conversation with my father weeks earlier when he asked me, out of context, who I'd want to live with if "your mother and I got divorced." I instinctively said "Mom," and he stormed off in a huff without comment. My mother had been a safe place all my life. It was an easy choice. I guess he didn't see it that way.

Evidently, Trey received the same question and chose my father, because when the two of them arrived at the house, Trey knew he was leaving. There was no discussion. He got his things and joined our father.

After Trey and my father left the house, I ran into the garage after them. My father was behind the wheel of his car with Trey in the passenger seat. They were about to drive off. I tapped on the driver's side window, and my father rolled it down.

I said, "Daddy, I just want you to know, I love you."

He looked dead at me while my words hung in the air for a few excruciating seconds. He then turned his eyes away, rolled up the window, put the car in gear, and backed out of the driveway. I stood there frozen, with a broken heart, and watched them disappear slowly down the road until they were out of sight.

Divorce quickly followed the unceremonious removal of my father from the Conway home. It was 1992, and I was fifteen. The picture-perfect family the outside world saw had come apart at the seams. I understood that parents got divorced. Still, it didn't seem to happen much in Conway, and I felt stigmatized as collateral damage in my parents' war. Yet, despite the emotional upheaval, I knew I had to make do. I had a life to lead. I got that much.

When the ink dried on the divorce papers, my father got the Shady Valley home—he would have gone down fighting to keep that house—meaning, my mother and I had to move. Mom managed to find a much smaller place in a little subdivision named Bainbridge, less than ten minutes away and south of the Country Club. The homes were walking distance apart, making it super easy for visits for estranged family—were they so inclined. They weren't.

The main thing, what kept my chin up, was that I came out fine in the custody split. By all indications, my father had become the problem. He had fueled the turbulence in our household and, more than anyone, I felt he should shoulder the blame for the family demise.

So, in the crease of silver linings, I came away with the parent who had a track record of making things right and showing unconditional love to her children. I felt I could count on Mom to prop me up, guide me and, when necessary, give me that reassuring hug.

I got the Rock of Gibraltar mother and Trey got the loose cannon. Advantage Ashley.

Better still, I no longer had to suffer a home that featured yelling and screaming as regular background music. In its place, I'd have peace, quiet, and stability, a return to normal.

You know what they say about best laid plans?

Almost immediately, my mother took a deep dive into the singles world. She started visiting Little Rock to party and hang out in various bars and survey the pickings. She enrolled at college, working toward a degree in dental hygiene. She worked at Chili's to generate cash flow to supplement alimony. She was trailblazing as a single woman with unrestrained vengeance.

I didn't entirely blame her. The poor thing got married to my father when she was a pregnant high school senior, two years older than I. She was entitled to break out. If nothing else, she deserved a meaningful respite from all the stormy years and a domestic role that afforded her little time for herself. She had a right to find her way. She, too, was collateral damage.

But as time would show, her game plan wasn't to just get something out of her system. Nor was it a transition to something more balanced. It was a major makeover, the new and improved Lark. And the new Lark didn't have parenting high on her to-do list. It was a narrowly focused take-care-of-me re-do. She was rarely around. She was either at college, working, or dating. I was left to deal on my own with the aftermath of a divorce, disassembly of our nuclear family, and the weirdness that came with teenage life.

And it got worse.

I remember the first time I saw her sloppy drunk. We were in Lake Powell, Arizona, visiting Aunt Gaye and Uncle Kevin, and by mid-afternoon my mom was plastered like I had never seen. She slurred words and struggled on her feet and laughed at the dumbest things. She was silly, stupid-drunk. Seeing her that way for the first time embarrassed and disturbed me.

It snowballed into a pattern.

On occasion I'd arrive home to find her totally shit-faced. It was as if she went into a phone booth as nurturing supermom and came out as wild party mom. The woman who occupied the bedroom next to mine looked, dressed, talked, and laughed like my mother. But that was where the resemblance ended. She had become a mere facsimile of the parental rock that once grounded my world.

Then the dating become incessant, like she was test-driving an assembly line of boyfriends for the next long-term mate. Most I couldn't stand. They were either gross, immature, or weird, a parade of losers so far as I could tell. As difficult as my father could be, and as angry at him as I was, none held a candle to Carter Elliott.

Free of parental restraints, I pushed my own boundaries. I began to flout my womanhood and numb my pain with drugs and alcohol. I wasn't getting any adult lessons, cautionary warnings, or advice. My father had taken a flyer on me and my mother had recalibrated how I fit into her world, downgrading me from daughter to girlfriend. We had become roommates for all intents and purposes.

Lacking parental controls and armed with an impetuous and increasingly untamed personality, I pretty much did what I wanted. I think my mom was aware of most, if not all, of what I did. She probably didn't know how to handle it. Besides, she had other priorities. If I came home alive, she was satisfied.

The discipline I so desperately needed was nowhere to be found.

I needed my dad. When he was able to tap into his parental soft spot, he could be loving, supportive, and wise. He didn't tolerate bullshit, and I knew he would protect me to the hilt. He might have traditional notions that didn't suit me, but he had a set of values he cherished and expected his children to embrace. I needed an adult in my life and, while not perfect by any stretch, he qualified.

And moving into his house would have mutual benefits. I'd have financial stability, a job like my brother at Dad's company, and all that my father promised me. I'd also have my protector closer by, which meant less drugs and alcohol. I thought it could benefit him too. My presence could inspire him to downshift on the partying he craved and the craziness in his life, make him more adult-responsible. And maybe if I moved out of my mother's house, she might feel like rebooting her adult life as well.

His world view was narrower. From his vantage point, my coming home would be a package deal, a way to manipulate my mother to return. He ran his life like he ran his business, always looking for a play. I felt like a pawn. I wasn't about to indulge my father. My reflections about a resurrected normal family had crashed and burned once again.

I resolved to leave Arkansas. I needed a clean break. Once free of high school, I wanted to enroll at Columbia College in Chicago to study art and film. I persuaded my mother to take me for a campus tour. I loved the place and beamed with excitement about the possibilities.

I needed financial help. I approached my father, and without so much as taking another breath, he dismissed the idea out of hand, as if swatting a pesky fly. He said I could never make a living with a liberal arts degree—"You'll never make any money doing that!"—and that I needed to readjust my career sights.

Translation: attend school locally and build a life in Arkansas.

Unstated rationale: stay in Conway to be near me.

It was his twisted version of a parental Catch-22. On the one hand, he didn't want to include me in his life like a father should and, on the other, didn't want me so removed he couldn't get an occasional fix to allay his guilt for not including me.

I appeased my father and enrolled at a local school, Hendrix College, and got my first taste of secondary education. I liked it, but the itch to haul my butt out of Arkansas persisted. I yearned for considerable distance from the Conway drama. I decided Utah should be the next stop. My Aunt Gaye and Uncle Kevin still lived in Bountiful, Utah, about ten miles north of Salt Lake City, the perfect cover for my plan. If I told my father I was pulling up stakes for an out-of-state destination, he'd have a shit fit. So I did what any self-respecting teenager would do: I lied.

I told my dad I was going to spend a week or two after my inaugural college experience to visit Aunt Gaye. Meanwhile, my mother and I planned my move. We loaded up my two-door Honda, my cat, and clothes, and I headed west. I found an apartment in Salt Lake City, got a job, enrolled in Salt Lake City Community College, and started a new life.

Once reestablished, I told my father the truth and, predictably, he flipped out and threatened to shut me out. Really? I think you have to be in before you can be out.

Things eventually calmed down, at least to the point where my father started speaking to me. My mother was pretty much off doing her thing. She relocated to Texas with her latest boyfriend. I visited Arkansas now and again, to see friends, party hard, and make obligatory visits to my father.

After two years at the local community college to get my generals and establish residency, I transferred to the University of Utah for a mainstream matriculated program, majoring in Communications. My life in Utah was inching toward normal.

Still, I desired my father in my life, which I kept undisclosed out of fear he'd reject me, adding another scar to the growing collection. We started slowly to reconnect, and he allowed me back "in." He bought me bedroom furniture and decorated my apartment. He started to visit when his business schedule allowed. I also saw him over the holidays.

Then we had a memorable visit when he and my mom came to see me. I had suffered a serious knee injury while mountain biking. I was homebound, and they took attentive care of me. It was refreshing to be parented, not only by one, but both my parents. It had been a while since I felt like the daughter I once was, if only for a few days.

During the visit, while hanging out one evening at my apartment, my parents got happily drunk. It was the first time since before the divorce I saw them enjoying each other. Sure, the alcohol gamed the moment, but they genuinely seemed pleased to be with each other. I couldn't help but wonder whether it was a one-time thing, a belt of booze-infused serendipity, or a preview of something more significant. I think, like many children of divorced parents, deep down I longed for a mending of the past and a return to the nuclear family unit. And while these musings didn't linger after we each returned to our routines, seeing a positive slice of the Lark and Carter Show of yesteryear gave me encouraging pause.

Life in Utah continued. I was moving toward my Communications degree and still making my way back to myself. In 1999, after liberally sampling the local social and dating market, I met Cory Furness, and we started dating to the point of an introduction to my parents. My mother said little about the relationship, but my father got a genuine kick out of Cory. He found him a source of entertainment, young blood he could attach as a sidekick for his partying dalliances, as he continued to chase the ghosts of his youth.

My father took Cory and me on trips, sometimes with his private plane. He took us to Las Vegas for shows and places to party. He brought us to Florida for a weekend of virtual non-stop partying. Like my mom, my father had begun to treat me like a friend he could take around and introduce and get wasted together, a social appendage.

The bro-fests my dad had with Cory helped increase my own social contact with my father, and I got to see him at his unadulterated worst. He was characteristically wild in social settings. Someone once said that he was the kind of guy who raises the temperature in a bar, stirs up shit for the heck of it, and gets his jaw broken for fun. Goddamn, what a great night out!

Once, while at a restaurant with him, a scantily clad, hot girl was circling with roses to sell. My father told her he'd buy the entire batch if she sat down to drink with us. She couldn't have been more than a year or two older than I was. It disgusted me, and I told him so later.

I witnessed my father do many disgraceful acts. In my typical style, I unloaded on him with an impassioned lecture about his hypocrisy, throwing in his face his constant, self-righteous religious platitudes and bible-thumping.

He would ogle how my girlfriends dressed and call me a slut if I dressed the same way. He'd get a kick out of how drunk a girlfriend was, but would give me hell for drinking too much. When I danced at a bar with a girlfriend, he went off on me, calling me a "fucking lesbian."

He would flirt with my girlfriends at dinner. He would invite younger women, sometimes from his office or a roommate of mine, to hang with us, not so I could have the company of a peer, but so he could make the moves on them.

He'd use me as his wingman, and when it became blatantly obvious, I'd go ballistic.

And so we fought, and half the time, he'd apologize, sometimes in tears. He confused and angered me. I didn't hate him, although it might have appeared that way. I struggled to understand and connect with him, to get clear on why he did the things he did. We had a steady flow of highs and lows, polar opposite swings that never rested in the middle.

Despite all the angst he gave me, things were improving between us. I was getting more stable and self-sufficient. I was working toward a college degree and had a steady boyfriend. I was coming into my own. No longer a child, I was starting to become an adult in the relationship. I knew what to expect from my father. Lowering my expectations of our relationship reduced my frustration and increased my tolerance.

I also knew he would always be there for me, despite the aggravation he thought I caused him, and his errant ways. When push came to shove, I knew I could count on him to show up as my father. Once, when I got whopping drunk in Utah at a party and thought I may have been raped—I hadn't—he immediately got on a plane to be with me.

My dad was untamed and immature. But I knew he loved me. He struggled to find his emotional outlet. I had hope. We would get there.

Then things took a turn for the truly peculiar.

3

ENTER RICHARD RALPH CONTE, M.D.

During this time, my Uncle Kevin Clark introduced Dick Conte to our lives. The two attended medical school together in the early '80s. Conte became an emergency room physician and Uncle Kevin a surgeon. They stayed in touch and developed a sustained friendship that stretched beyond their medical world, including taking hunting trips together. Aunt Gaye, my mother's sister, and Uncle Kevin often invited Conte to their social events, which is how my mother met him.

To put it mildly, from the start I was not a big fan of the guy. He was socially ill-equipped and didn't have a personality to write home about. He said little, at least when I was around, and seemed uncomfortable in his own skin and sometimes a little creepy. Physically, he was, well, not from central casting.

Most bizarre was how Conte boasted he was a contract mercenary, working for a private entity (Vinnell Corporation) under federal contract to supplement US armed forces in faraway exotic places like Grenada and Afghanistan. Someone in the family mentioned once that Conte was a trained sniper and that he had spent time providing medical support to the SWAT team at the Carson City Sheriff's Office in Nevada. He wore military boots as his signature footwear, often wore combat fatigues, read military magazines, and collected weapons. He walked with a limp, which he blamed on a shrapnel wound courtesy of the Vietnam War.

Over time, Mom and Conte got chummier, so much so that in early July 2000, my mother moved from Houston to Salt Lake City to be closer to him. I thought the reason was to be near me since I lived in Salt Lake at the time. While that might have influenced her, the main reason was better access to Conte, who lived in Carson City, Nevada and had a place in Duck Creek, Utah. In the blur of months, they upped their relationship a few romantic pegs.

For the life of me, I couldn't see what my mom saw in him. But I didn't make waves. I knew my materialistic mother. Even though she was a professional in her own right as a dental hygienist, she wanted someone to take care of her, and by early indications, Conte had requisite resources. He was a successful ER doctor and owned substantial properties in Nevada and Utah.

Their burgeoning relationship triggered a series of events that changed the landscape.

In January 2001, my mother moved some things from Texas to Utah, and Conte and I helped her unload and carry boxes. During a break in the hauling of things, while Conte and I stood outside the condo milling about, out of the blue he said that if I ever wanted to kill somebody, the key was to put the body in a black plastic garbage bag with heavy chains and locks and dump the secure package into a deep body of water. After the splash, he emphasized, the bag would sink to the bottom and remain there for all time. Thank you, Dick, for that invaluable career advice.

In February 2001, my mother broke off her relationship with Conte. From what I could tell, she awoke one day and said to herself, "Enough of this, I am done with him." That is how my mother rolled. She had many fish in the sea to catch if she wanted, and it appeared that once again, the talented and beautiful Lark wanted to put her fish hook back in the water.

In May, I proudly graduated from the University of Utah with a B.A. in Communications. I didn't attend the ceremony, opting instead to attend the wedding of my best friend Ann.

In June, my mother and Conte resurrected their relationship. To my knowledge, there was no apparent rhyme or reason. Again, it was Lark rolling as Lark did.

In July, while visiting Lake Powell one weekend with my mom, Conte, and Cory, I mentioned that Cory and I were pondering engagement. I don't recall my mother's specific reaction other than, on the spectrum of emotive responses, it was close to "Ho-hum," as in "That's nice."

Later that same weekend, to raise us one, Conte showed us a fresh bullet wound in his back that he claimed he got while on a military mission for Vinnell Corporation and the US government. Yeah, I thought, this is going to last.

To show how much I knew, not long thereafter, my mother announced that she and Conte planned to marry. Great. I was half-shocked, half-whatever. I was learning that when it came to my parents, expect the worst, and celebrate if they underachieve.

I knew the deal. My mom thought the guy had money, and despite the blazing red flags, that sealed it for her. I did what any loving daughter in this situation would do. I didn't argue. "Fine. Your decision. I wash my hands of this weirdness. Good luck. Oh, and congratulations."

Not a ringing endorsement, but not my signature outrage either. In fact, given that, in typical Lark fashion she stole my engagement thunder, I think I was remarkably restrained.

Sure enough, on October 17, at a civil ceremony at St. Vincent and the Grenadines, a tiny country in the Caribbean, my mother and Conte got married. It was a small gathering that didn't include family. No offense taken.

Two weeks later, on October 31, fittingly Halloween, I reclaimed my thunder when Cory and I got engaged. It turns out, to his absolute credit, before formally offering me the ring, and unknown to me,

Cory asked my father for my hand in marriage. I hadn't pegged Cory as that noble, but he was, and I found that sweet.

Cory had taken an unknown risk, unaware my father had directed me not to marry Cory because he lacked initiative, a euphemism for lazy. But my father, to my surprise, said yes, and all was good in the world. My mom extended obligatory congratulations in her inimitable way. Hard to get a rise out her. We set the happy date for October 12, 2002.

I didn't realize it at the time, but once Cory and I got engaged and we began to make wedding plans, my parents, by default, had to speak to each other more than normal. It was the nature of the beast: Parents had to be involved, decisions had to be made. The engagement brought them a little closer, a small item that I'm betting wasn't lost on Conte.

On December 1, 2001, in the British West Indies, my mother and Conte staged a formal church wedding with all family present, save my brother who boycotted the event, I am sure out of allegiance to my father. The church ceremony, for family and legal purposes, made it official. Dick Conte was my stepfather. Lucky me.

At the wedding, I danced with Conte—an act of unparalleled bravery—and as we uneasily shuffled through the music, he whispered that Trey and I need never worry, he would always take care of and protect my mother, and that if we ever needed anything, he would be there for us. He sounded like he really meant it.

That weekend my mother visited Conte's Carson City home for the first time. They had not moved in together, continuing their long-distance romance. It shocked her. The place looked as if a tornado had swept through the home of a reclusive pack rat and wreaked untold havoc. The place also was decorated with weapons. It also came armed with hidden surveillance cameras that captured on film everything people did while there, including in the spare bedroom.

It was a jaw-dropping visual—and a wake-up call for my mother. What had she done?

In early February, Dad took my roommate and me to Las Vegas for a weekend. He brought his protégé, Timmy Wayne Robertson, to help occupy my time. As I normally did, before going to sleep, I took my engagement ring off and placed it on the bedside table. The next morning, when I frantically couldn't find it, my father matter-of-factly explained he pawned the damn thing to advance his gambling agenda the night before. I went off on him like I had never done before. One step forward, several back with him. I got the ring back.

On February 25, 2002, less than three months after the church wedding, my mother told Conte she wasn't happy in the marriage and wanted out. He sobbed like a child, baffled she could do that after professing her love so passionately on Valentine's Day and via countless prior emails that waxed all ways romantic.

His bewilderment was understandable. During their short time together, to say that my mother had laid it on a bit thick would be the depth of understatement. What else could the guy think other than he had found the romantic prize of a lifetime? He had reason to feel she had thrown him out with the garbage. Conte begged her to change her mind. She didn't budge. Lark was rolling again.

In early March, despite the hammer that had come down on him, Conte allowed Cory and me access to his cabin in Duck Creek, Utah for a weekend away. But before we left, my mother told me that Cory and I should not have sex at the cabin. Why, Mom? Because Conte had cameras hidden there, and we'd find ourselves starring in our own porn film and gifting Conte free adult entertainment. Could this get any weirder?

As we were driving to Duck Creek, my father called with bad news. His father had died. I felt compassion for him and asked him if he wanted me to end the trip and jump on a plane to attend funeral services. He said, no, it was okay, brushing it off less than convincingly. I didn't go, which in hindsight I am betting upset him. But I lived in Utah and the funeral was in Arkansas, at least that was one way I justified my selfishness. I also hadn't been close to his family since my parents' divorce, which while true, was another self-serving contrivance. I was thinking only of myself.

Over the next several weeks, I began to realize that, even though I was the daughter and not the designated adult in the relationship, I had to stop standing on ceremony. I had to start acting like the daughter I wanted him to treat me as. I had to grow up more.

My wedding plans continued. I wanted a big wedding, and while my father didn't want to pay for a big wedding, I eventually prevailed upon him. I also wanted this expensive Vera Wang gown as my wedding dress, which priced out at ten thousand dollars, and that was for a sample garment. My father couldn't wrap his mind around the notion of spending ten grand for a dress I'd wear once in my life. I was neither mad at my father nor upset. As a matter of logic, I couldn't quarrel. But I was starring in the role of princess. I wanted the dress. He said "no,"—well, not expressly. He wisely hemmed and hawed, allowing the discussion to float about without closure, presumably hoping I'd come to my senses without him having to shut the door.

I didn't come to my senses. I found the money instead or, more to reality, it found me. Somehow—I wonder how, Mom—Conte got wind of the dress dilemma and stepped up to pay for the gown. Damn, my mother had this guy under her spell. Even though Conte and my mother were separated and I couldn't stand the guy, I didn't hesitate to grab the money. Score one for personal integrity.

On April 13, 2002, Cory and I celebrated our engagement at the Market Street Oyster Bar in Salt Lake City, Utah. My mother didn't invite Conte. Understandable. My father, who had agreed to pay for half of the gala, didn't bring his girlfriend. Less understandable. My parents both attended, unattached.

Maybe I should have sensed it coming, but the most memorable takeaway of the party was how intimately my parents got along. They danced and drank together and hung all over each other the entire night, as if they were the ones getting hitched. They got along so well that my father wound up paying for the entire event. I couldn't help but wonder, again—is there a reconciliation in the offing? In the parking lot at the end of the party, word circulated that my parents were making out. I was too drunk to care or let it register in the moment.

Word also reached us via the rumor mill from an unknown source, although at one point it was attributed to an unspecified FBI agent, that the uninvited Conte had lurked in the parking lot shadows during the party, spying on us. The party had taken place both indoors in a hall and outdoors on a patio. He easily could surveil anything that happened outside, especially with his military-grade binoculars, including an up-close and almost personal visual of my parents carrying on in the parking lot like teenagers in heat.

I again began to wonder about my parents getting back together. Was that wishful thinking? Was I reading too much into what happened at the party? They were drunk and it was a happy occasion. And, Lord knows, they weren't patron saints of behavioral boundaries.

My musings brought me back to an early December morning episode shortly after Mom and I started living in Bainbridge. At the time, the ink on my parents' divorce was still wet, and my mom and I were licking our wounds trying to figure out the new life we were about to have, she as a divorcée and I as the fifteen-year-old daughter of divorced parents. I was on my way to school in a car with a classmate. When we arrived at a four-way stop sign, I looked up to see a giant billboard on the street corner emblazoned with "Lark and Ashley, please come home for Christmas."

Holy shit! My father had broadcast to the entire city of Conway his irrepressible desire for reconciliation, a month after the divorce became final. A friend of his owned the land and no doubt had given him access to make the domestic promo pitch. The city of Conway was small enough and my father's prominence as a businessman pervasive enough that most knew my parents.

I was mortified, as was my mother. It was a gargantuan public embarrassment. When my mother found out, she purchased cans of spray paint and blackened the message.

The billboard stunt was so my father. He hated to lose, hated it, and he had lost the game as a husband and as a father. He had failed. But he also felt he could manipulate almost any situation for a win. He couldn't stand being away from my mother, and struggled to deal with life without *his* wife. And the billboard wouldn't be the only bloated display of his desperation. A few months later, he sent her 365 roses. It was the kind of thing that Conte would do—and often did—with my mom. Irony of ironies?

Despite the embarrassment I felt back then, looking back with more maturity and my own marriage on the horizon, I could find the sweet spots in those inflated romantic gestures. Maybe my parents never fell out of love. Maybe the behavior at the engagement party held a clue as to how they now felt toward each other?

Four days after our engagement party, on April 17, my mother drew up formal divorce papers for her and Conte on the basis of a consensual parting of the ways. Divorce by consent greases the system, saving money and reducing stress. She didn't want to prolong the process.

Shortly thereafter, my mother presented the papers to Conte for his signature. He didn't want to sign. He didn't want a divorce and, in any event, it wasn't consensual. Not a problem. She picked up her fiddle and played it, asking him, I'm sure with seductively poisonous eyes, if he wanted to keep her in a marriage that made her unhappy, a rhetorical question if ever there was one. He sheepishly said no and signed the papers. When it came to men, Mom was virtuoso.

A week later, on Wednesday, May 15, 2002, I called my father from my job at Vanguard Media Group to chat. I took the opportunity to go off a little on Conte, and how he was so wacko. The signed divorce papers he'd returned to my mom were interspersed with romantic notes and accompanied by flowers. The night he delivered them, he insisted on taking her to dinner, for one final "date." A few days later, he snuck into my mom's apartment—he had the combination to the lock—and put romantic cards all over her house. He also sent roses to her at work. Conte struggled with reading the writing on a wall. My dad didn't comment.

We also discussed my wedding. I told him how much I was looking forward to him walking me down the aisle. I had worried about asking him to perform that traditional fatherly role, which normally would go without saying, but my anxiety reflected the continued tenuous nature of our relationship and his avowed disapproval of my future spouse. I was also afraid he would reject me again. I assumed, too, he knew that if he tried to stand in the way, then we'd elope like he and my teenaged pregnant mom did, thus leaving him offstage for a major event in the life of his only daughter. Dad didn't like being offstage.

I also mentioned that Cory and I had plans for the upcoming weekend, May 18 and 19, to go to Wendover, a resort near the Nevada and Utah shared border, to gamble and golf and take a break from wedding planning and our lives in general. He wished us a good time away. We both promised to catch up the following week. It was a sweet conversation.

My life had slivers of sunlight beaming down on me, and the future looked brighter than it had in a long time. I was getting married. The chance to belong to a large family who loved and accepted me thrilled me. Mom seemed to have severed ties with Conte. He and all his strangeness were fading from our lives. My relationship with my father, while still needing major repair, was finding a groove. My parents, divorced for a decade now, might be finding their way back to each other. While more work unquestionably had to be done there, I giggled at the notion that reconciliation was even a rational concept.

As I pondered the many recent changes, I felt a rush of joy, a depth of feeling I hadn't felt since the breezy days of Greenbriar. I was twenty-five years old and excited about what life had in store for me.

4

LATE IN THE AFTERNOON OF Sunday, May 19, Cory and I returned home from a weekend of gambling, golf, and drinking at Wendover. While the Wendover diversion seemed like a good idea at the time, in truth, I despised gambling and didn't like to golf. And while I could always get up for drinking, and did my fair share that weekend, I didn't need to take a trip for that indulgence. I was eager to resume weekly routines and look forward to the new vistas in my life.

After settling back in at home, Cory and I went outside to bask in the unusually hot May weather, as the temperatures stayed consistent in the high 80s late into the afternoon. We lived in a rented basement unit of a private home. We loved the place. It was located high on a hill and from the backyard where we were relaxing, we had a breathtaking view of Salt Lake City.

As the sun began to go down, my mother telephoned. She said she wanted to make sure I was home because she was coming over right away. She abruptly hung up. What was I supposed to make of that?

I recalled that my mother had an appointment that day with a local attorney. I surmised that the meeting went sideways, and she wanted to talk about it. She had a penchant for drama, so I didn't get bent out of shape by the tone in her voice or the abruptness of the hang-up.

Whatever it was, I figured it was another tricky day in the life of Lark Elliott, which I could handle when she showed up. She lived close and I expected her in ten or less minutes. I went inside to wait.

When I heard the familiar sounds of her footsteps, I went into the hallway to greet her. She opened the door and took a few steps inside before coming to an unsteady halt. She had on a disturbingly sad face, a look I'd never seen on her before. She said nothing.

I said, "Who died?" My question matched her look.

She looked at me, holding back tears.

She said, "Oh, Ashley."

I thought Poppy, my grandfather and Mom's father, had died. He was up in years and hadn't been well. His time had arrived.

"Was it Poppy?" I said. She struggled to speak. She looked anguished.

"Who died?" I said in a raised voice.

"Oh, Ashley," she repeated.

I looked at her, trying to extract an answer from her face. She spared me the guesswork.

"It's your Dad."

I dropped to my knees like a heavy sack. I felt I had received a swift and powerful kick to the stomach. I began to cry, in incoherent bursts, with labored breathing, which quickly turned into uncontrollable heaving sobs. I couldn't stop. I became hysterical. I started to scream, while my mother stood at my feet, trying to provide details. I heard the word "robbery," but virtually nothing else. I wasn't paying her much mind. I was reeling from the news, that my father was dead—murdered, to be exact.

I began to scream at my mother. "Where's Dick?! Where's Dick?!"

She didn't say anything.

"Where the fuck is he?!" I was screaming loudly. "You need to call him." I could feel my eyes bulging. I must have looked insane. I yelled at her again. "Where the fuck is he?"

She assured me he was at his cabin in Duck Creek.

I had become fixated instantly on the possibility that Dick Conte had a hand in this. He was a self-professed trained killer. He had more than ample means to kill. He boasted know-how in getting rid of a dead body. He was a nut job. I mean, what does that tell you?

I continue to pummel my mother with demands to call Conte to learn what she could. She promised me she would.

I was utterly distraught and didn't know what to do with myself. Virtually everything that occurred in the next few hours, after I got the news, is blacked out. It is so odd. I probably talked to my brother, but I have no such memory. What would we have discussed? I probably sat with my mom, but after she played bad news messenger, I have no memory of her staying and I am not sure she would have been much help anyway. I must have talked with Cory—that would seem the natural thing to do—but whatever we discussed I can't recall.

I finally connected with my best friend, Ann, in Arkansas. She had been trying to reach me. Ann was aware of the news, and in fact knew before I did, as local media in Little Rock was all over it. We both struggled to make it real. Since she had seen the news, I wanted details. There weren't too many.

It was a double homicide, apparently the first in Conway history. Whoever killed my father also killed my friend and Dad's protégé, Timmy Wayne Robertson. Timmy Wayne was twenty-five, like me, and worked at Detco Industries, my father's business.

An intruder had gotten inside the house, either late the night of May 18 or during the wee hours of the morning of May 19, and killed both my father and Timmy Wayne in the front room of the house, each with a single bullet to the head while they lay face down on the carpet. TV news characterized the homicides as a hit, an execution-style killing, with my father as the sole target. Timmy Wayne was collateral damage, in the wrong place at the wrong time.

My father's girlfriend, Christie Jameson, discovered the bodies in the early evening of May 19. Christie had come over to use the pool, which had been recently renovated in anticipation of a big summer party my father had planned to throw in the ensuing weeks. Christie walked in, saw the bodies, and ran out of the house screaming for help.

That was as much as the media knew. The police I assumed knew more.

I told Ann I was coming to Arkansas on the earliest flight and I would see her tomorrow. I tried to get some sleep. I don't remember if I did. I was in an ongoing fog, in and out of consciousness. When I awoke hours later, I had a few seconds of normalcy before realizing that my father had been murdered. I fell into deep depression.

One memory I do have that I can't shake is packing for the trip to Arkansas. I remember trying to untangle wire hangers to get the clothes I wanted. The battle with the metal hangers has become an image tattooed in my mind, a curse for the rest of my life. Wire hangers constantly remind me of what I want to forget, forever associated with my father's death.

But after packing, I remember virtually nothing more in the aftermath of the news.

I don't remember making travel arrangements. I don't remember my flight from Utah to Arkansas. I don't remember arriving at the Little Rock airport. And I don't recall Ann picking me up from the flight.

I don't remember the crying I did when she held me at the airport. I don't remember that during the ride from the airport to the Shady Valley house, I behaved more angry than distraught. I don't remember how Ann and I shared, again and again, our utter disbelief at what had happened. I don't remember that Cory came with me.

How does someone forget these things? I would have thought they'd be ingrained in the psyche. Are the memories lost for all time? Can they be recovered, like deleted emails?

My memory picks up when we arrived at the Shady Valley home on May 20 in the early afternoon. After Ann dropped me off, I trudged toward the garage entrance. I was in a zombie-like state. I didn't know what to expect, except lots of police. But as I got out Ann's car I was surprised at what I saw. There were no police squad cars. There was no yellow tape around the home. There were no policeman, detectives, or investigators anywhere to be found. It was slightly more than twenty-four hours since Christie Jameson had discovered the bodies. And normalcy had returned?

The collection of evidence couldn't possibly be over, could it? Where was law enforcement? Why weren't they interviewing the people in the house? What was going on? Was this an ill-conceived, cruel prank? Is my father about to jump out of the garage, laughing hysterically about how he fooled everyone and played us all for suckers? My father had a well-earned reputation as a practical joker, and I wouldn't put it past him to do something colossally beyond the pale. But seriously, even he wouldn't go this far. Still, something didn't seem right.

I was to some degree in a state of shock. I didn't want to believe what was happening. I kept wanting someone to tell me it wasn't true, that a bad mistake had been made. Denial gets you through a few minutes here and there. It fuels imagination.

I walked into the house through the garage. My father's family was there—uncles, aunts, and cousins. Why were they there? What were all these people doing in my father's house? I honestly couldn't fathom why they had collected there. It was a crime scene, for crying out loud. But did it look like a crime scene? The bodies were gone, the evidence taken. Everything seemed to be in place, where it normally was, as if nothing had occurred, except the piano. It had been moved to allow the police to remove the hallway carpet which, I'd learned, was soaked with blood and had to go.

I stared at the once-carpeted naked floor and saw spots of blood. I had to concentrate to keep myself from throwing up. Was it my father's blood or Timmy Wayne's? Did it matter?

The police, I would learn, had inspected the property and promptly released the home back to the family. I didn't understand that. I was confused.

My dad's older brother, Rusty, approached me and we hugged. I cried and cried. I went into the kitchen. People hugged and greeted me, including my brother. I kept saying to myself, *why is everyone here? Isn't this a murder scene?* Are the police done, leaving us to hang out at Dad's place? It felt strange. We were at a party, but the party died the day before.

My mother wasn't there. I wondered if she would show up.

My head was spinning. The whole thing was surreal. I was overwhelmed and tormented. I felt stranded on an island with crazy thoughts, deep pain that wouldn't go away, and wholesale wariness.

I couldn't stay. I had to get away from everyone. I wanted to be in the house alone. I needed to return another time, when everyone was gone. I left.

I got in touch with Ann, and the two of us returned by ourselves at dusk, when the place had been evacuated. We awkwardly walked through the house. I felt abnormally timid and cautious, like I was in a haunted house I'd never visited before, and from the look on her face, Ann felt the same way. I was looking for signs of life, not human life, but things that pumped life back into the present, things I could hold onto, at least until I found my bearings.

I shuffled into my father's bedroom and fixed my eyes on the closet doors. I knew my father organized his regularly dry-cleaned garb like militia in formation. The closet contents would reveal a colorful and fastidious display of the looks my father had in public—his cool jeans, stylish boots and other expensive shoes, embroidered belts, and favorite shirts—each item at attention, awaiting the call of duty.

As soon as I opened the closet door, I regretted the move. His clean and pressed clothes were all there, hanging inside plastic bags, resting in orderly free flow, as expected. But keeping them afloat was an army of wire hangers! For me, it was a double whammy. Metal hangers and I locked in a painful destiny.

Before leaving the bedroom, I took a few things. My father liked white, button-down-collared shirts with his embroidered initials. I liked him better in blue to accentuate his sparkling blue eyes. I took a blue shirt as a keepsake.

I found the outfit he had worn to my engagement party. He had taken the sign off the door that said "Furness–Elliott Party," and stuffed it into the jacket pocket. I took that, too.

I commandeered a bottle of cologne I had bought for him. It was the last gift I gave him.

I took his reading glasses. They were crooked. They always were, which is how they sat on his face. It gave him a scholarly look, softening his edges, and diffusing his signature intimidation.

I lay in his bed to detect his scent. It was faint, but there, and I took it in. I wondered if he was asleep when the perpetrator arrived. Would I ever know? As I lay there, I had this pang in my heart about never enjoying his natural scent ever again. I wanted it to last. I had an idea.

My father had two closets in his bathroom. When I opened one closet, there were his dirty clothes, scattered on the floor. He'd had a habit of throwing stuff in there in lieu of a hamper. I immediately scooped up the jumbled pile and inhaled the air around the clothes to smell the scent. I cried. I took them all as a tangible reminder of my father as a physical being. I still have the clothes. The scent is long gone.

After generating my collection, I settled with Ann into the kitchen, the safe place for all homes. Ann and I reviewed what little we knew about what went down. The police investigation had started, of course, but who know where it would lead, if anywhere?

While we chatted in the kitchen, I grabbed the handle of the under-the-counter pull-out drawer that contained the garbage disposal, to throw something out. I looked in and on top saw a crumpled Taco Bell receipt. It looked fresh. It had a date stamp of May 18. I turned it over to the local police.

I remained baffled by how quickly local police turned the property back over to the family. I had asked earlier whether investigators had vacuumed the home for evidence of dog hairs. They had not. Conte owned two dogs, and he never went anywhere without them. If he had something to do with this, the dogs likely were his sidekicks. Did they leave evidence of their presence? The floors might hold the answer. The police agreed to vacuum the place.

Earlier in the evening, while scanning my father's bedroom, I had sat on the chaise lounge next to his bed. I was discussing something with Ann when at some point, I leaned back and felt a lump behind the pillow. I reached back and found a handgun. Wow. Was my father trying to figure out a way to grab the gun? Did he even have the chance? How much time transpired between when the intruder confronted him and he got shot? Did any of these questions matter?

I called my brother to let him know about the gun. I later gave it to him to give to local police. I began to get eager about the criminal investigation.

About two hours into our self-guided tour of the Shady Valley house, as darkness draped the neighborhood, Ann and I heard a suspicious noise outside. Someone was trying to enter the house through the locked front door. We instinctively cast each other alarmed and frightened looks. We became still and listened. The front door noise stopped. We heard footsteps. A few seconds later, we saw a shadow around the side of the house moving toward the garage entrance. When the shadow approached at the glass bay window, its owner came into full view.

It was my mother!

After letting her in, I let her have it. "You can't do that!" I screamed. "You freaked us the fuck out."

At this point, to our knowledge, the criminal investigation hadn't focused on specific suspects, although it wouldn't take long. For now I assumed it was open season, and no one had a bead on who killed my father and Timmy Wayne. For all we knew, whoever did it might return to the scene of the crime in search of something they'd forgotten, especially if they'd heard the police had released the house back to the family. The house contained many precious items, including money and jewelry I assumed, and who knew what else might pique perpetrator interest. That someone, during darkness, lurked outside when no one was expected, naturally shook us up.

I had to explain all this to my mother, who apologized, gave me and Ann hugs, and joined us in the kitchen. As we hung out, my mother kept saying repeatedly that she couldn't believe what had happened. Then she started flashing to this and that memory, and telling stories about my father and our family: Remember when we did this Ashley? Remember when your father did that? It made me uncomfortable. One day earlier someone had found the dead body of my father with a bullet in his head about thirty feet from where we were standing, so it seemed way too early to reminiscence. The day before! Right over there! Don't we get to grieve and feel like shit before we wax nostalgic? Isn't that what normal people do? Can we feel miserable for a day or two before we get on with the business of celebrating the life?

To me, in my altered state, her professed longing was conspicuously odd, as if she were trying to tell us something, wanting to be heard. The more she talked, the more removed I became and the more her voice became fuzzy and distant. I began to wonder, *How was it she showed up in darkness at the home without alerting anyone? How did she expect to get in? Why did she come alone? What was her purpose in coming at this late hour? Was she looking to find something in the house? What would she have done if we hadn't been here?*

My mother could be eccentric and unpredictable. But this seemed out of character even for her. She continued to spew memories, the words no longer heard, and as she did, she struck me as a performer alone on a performance stage, the kitchen lights casting her in a silhouette, self-absorbed and exposed, delivering the final monologue of a one-act tragedy.

My thoughts became spooky, super spooky, and I thought, *Yes, indeed that is one sick notion.* But was it conceivable? Stranger things have happened.

5

THE NEXT MORNING, TUESDAY, MAY 21, I awoke to a drowsy
sense of being somewhere unknown. I gazed though narrow slits in my
eyelids at the foreign walls and furniture. I was in an unrecognizable
room lying on an unfamiliar bed. In seconds, reality hit hard. I was
in a Howard Johnson's hotel in Conway, Arkansas—and my father
was dead.

I became consumed with sadness. I held back tears. I felt numb
except for the heaviness in my heart. I dreaded what lay in store for
me in a couple of hours. I'd soon face a dispiriting cluster of funeral-
related tasks and the prospects of dealing with family.

It went downhill from there.

I arrived at the funeral home to discover a large group of family
and friends assembled together, twenty or more. What was up with
that? I was there to get with my brother to make funeral arrangements.
Why did we need a small army for the few things we could and should
handle?

I guess I didn't hide my surprise and disgust, which explained the
sneers and smirky glances I got in return. Not the best start.

I inserted myself. I told funeral parlor staff I wanted to see my
father before we did anything further, that is, before they did what

funeral home people do to prepare a body for open casket viewing. I told them I wanted to see him before they put their hands on him.

The heads of the assembled mourners swiveled and bobbed at each other with disbelieving looks. I'd seen the looks before. There she goes again. That girl is batshit, always was, always will be. I wanted to take a bow.

The funeral people spoke first, telling me that my father's head was swollen and disfigured and he didn't look like himself. They were firm but polite. They tried to reason with me, explaining that seeing him in the current condition wasn't a great idea. They paused, expecting me to understand.

Of course he didn't look like himself! He was dead for fuck sake. Okay, I didn't say those things, but that is what echoed loudly in my mind.

I stood my ground, insisting on seeing him the way he was right then. I didn't care how he looked. I knew he got shot in the head. I was prepared for that, or so I thought.

Family members chimed in, siding with the funeral folks, each saying a variation on the same theme: that neither I nor anyone else for that matter wanted to see my father that way and that I should stop this insanity. "That isn't how it's done, Ashley." "There are protocols." "They know what they're doing." "Let the funeral people do their job."

Leave well enough alone. Get over yourself.

I was upsetting them. They were getting agitated.

I didn't comprehend the problem. If no one wanted to see my father the way he was, fine by me. Their choice. They could stay while I went in the other room. Besides, I am his daughter, one of his only two children. I have some rights here, don't I? My feelings matter, don't they?

They kept pushing back. Fuck, I thought. What is with these people? But I knew. It was all too familiar. Everyone knew what was good for me except me. The untamed Ashley needed harnessing. I suppressed the urge to barge into the back room and let the chips fall.

The episode exhausted me. I felt overwhelmed, isolated, and

unsupported. I was fighting a losing battle and lacked the energy to push back. I relented with a crushed spirit.

The discussion caused someone to broach how to handle casket viewing. Should it be an open or closed coffin? Someone I didn't know kept saying that unless she got to see the body in an open casket, she wouldn't accept that my father was dead. She was adamant.

I was beside myself. *You crazy bitch* I thought, *my father is dead and you need proof? We need a coroner's inquest specially for you? Who are you anyway?*

I wanted an open coffin, too, but not for that reason. I wanted to see my dad one more time before I couldn't anymore.

Everyone had two cents to offer. People talked over the top of each other. This was fast becoming a nightmare. I glanced at my dad's two brothers and sister. I understood why they were there. I didn't mind hearing what they had to say. But this was, or should be, my and Trey's deal. Dad was ours, not theirs, wasn't he? I, not they, was Daddy's little girl. He was my protector, not theirs. It was my job to protect him from everyone in that room. I knew he'd want me to do that. I knew he'd want me to stand up for him.

So I opened my mouth again. I said that I didn't see how the opinions of the assembled mattered. Why didn't everyone let Trey and me figure out things and "you can go on with the rest of your day. We appreciate the help, but we got this." Or words to that effect.

The funeral planning process was to me surreal.

I was outnumbered. I didn't stand much of a chance. They did let me select what my father wore in his coffin. It wasn't much of a concession. I knew better than anyone, save perhaps my mom (who wasn't there), what outfits my father favored, what looks gave him an extra bounce in his step. Throw the crazy girl a bone, and maybe she'll stop flapping her gums.

I knew that from their perspective, I was a royal pain in the ass. I had a well-earned reputation for being difficult and harsh, an in-your-face kind of gal. A career in government diplomacy wasn't in my future. My prickly personality, current emotional condition, and disdain for several of those present, had merged to become my perfect toxic storm.

In my defense, that I was an emotional time-bomb didn't mean I was completely irrational. They were preempting my sorrow and dismissing my stifling despair with their fake concerns and self-righteous intrusion. *Didn't they understand how hard this was for me? No, they didn't. How could any of them possibly be in as much pain as I was?* I cannot imagine they were. *And who were these people to me, anyway?*

I began to have crazy thoughts again.

I peered at Trey. Why was he sporting Dad's diamond Rolex and diamond ring, and driving his car? Our father had just died and it felt like I had to prepare for a battle with my brother over my dad's belongings. I was in no way ready for that. Despite my lingering shock, from appearances at least, I might have to brace myself for a battle over material things down the road. Trey had his life and I had mine. But my sincere hope was that we could come together now, when we needed each other the most. The way he was talking (or I was hearing) was as if he was running our Dad's company. Had that happened? I started having crazy thoughts. *You couldn't wait until we buried him to lay claim to his expensive toys and take over his business? What was that all about? You had much to gain from Dad's death. Is there something you aren't telling me?*

I know how immature and self-centered this all sounds. And mean spirited. I make no excuses. I admit my failings. Call it a drama-queen outbreak if you like. But those were the thoughts and feelings I had. I struggled to come to grips with how everyone had insinuated themselves into the funeral and memorial arrangements. When my dad was alive, many of the same people in the room had dismissed him as reckless and irresponsible. Now they were all over his life in death. I wondered what they had to gain.

I was emotionally ill-equipped for what was happening. I hated everybody and wanted them to disappear. Too many cooks in the kitchen and too much bullshit. I was losing interest in whatever else had to be done. I said under my breath to myself, *Fuck it, I am out of here. Go ahead the rest of you, plan the funeral of my father and pick out the coffin and its interior and whatever else needs to happen in these hallowed halls. I surrender.*

Later that day, my brother and I selected the headstone and bought the cemetery plot. The self-appointed guardians of the process had no interest in that project. Thank the Lord. Trey and I bought six spots in the dirt if memory serves. I figured I'd bury my mom next to my dad whether she liked it or not. She would be dead. She won't be able to complain. Fancy that.

The rest of the day was a blur. I hung out with Ann and drank. I kept a stash of vodka in my room at Trey's place, which came in handy because Faulkner County, where Conway sat, was a dry county. The booze helped numb the pain. I don't even know how long I was there. Trey self-medicated with sleeping pills and crashed. I got drunk and he got to rest. He should have shared the pills.

The drinking numbed me. It also induced self-pity. One moment I felt nothing and the next I felt like a pathetic pile of misery. It reminded me of my relationship with my father. We swung hard from one extreme to the other, rarely stopping to rest at the happy middle. I could have gone for a dose of happy middle.

I wouldn't get any the next day.

6

ON WEDNESDAY, MAY 22, I had a hairdresser appointment. Before coming to Arkansas on Monday, my limited presence of mind included asking Ann to book me a time with the folks who did her hair. If I was going to my father's funeral, I wanted to do him proud in how I looked.

Ann dropped me off about noon. The staff knew who I was and why I was there. They had a cold bottle of Chardonnay available and asked if I'd like some. Guess what I said.

Two hours later, my hair was done, and I was certifiably drunk.

Ann retrieved me and we drove to the funeral home. The family had decided not to stage a public viewing, only a private, open-casket viewing for family. I was fine with that. When we arrived, Alan Duke was there. Duke, in his late thirties, wasn't family. He was a businessman who my father told me owed my father a sizeable amount of dinero. I never trusted the guy, and he'd soon find his way onto my initial personal shortlist of murder suspects. And not only because of money he might have owed my father. Other scintillating details emerged.

He descended upon Trey and me for chit-chat. We got the benevolence speech. He promised to take care of us. We'd never have to worry about money. He'd always be there for us. I felt so reassured he was in our corner. Like Dick Conte promised he'd be.

The funeral parlor staff came in and invited a select group to go the room with the open coffin. I recall Trey, my mother, my father's three siblings, me, and our pastor. There may have been others. I pulled Ann to come. I needed support, and she was the person to provide it.

Entering, I saw my dad across the way, lying still on his back, eyes closed, wearing the clothes I picked out for him. Dead.

My mom surged in front of everyone and put her wedding ring in the pocket of his jacket, as if the ring now meant something to her. I knew better. It was a grandstand move. She had long buried that ring deep in a drawer all these years. I had asked her for it more than once after she and my father divorced. I wanted to preserve its sentimental value as part of family legacy. Each time I asked, she flatly refused without explanation. Now, on the heels of my father's death, she fished the ring out as a prop for a command performance, entombing it for all time. *Way to go, Mom.*

That little move on her part got me going. I stormed to the coffin. As I got close, I totally freaked out. I started screaming. The funeral home person-in-charge tried to calm me. I tore into her, yelled that she had done a "fucking awful job." My father had on peach lipstick and his shade was all wrong. What had they done? I hardly recognized him. He looked like a drag queen!

"You made him look like—" I stopped, searching for words. "He's a fucking peach! He's a fucking peach! Why does he look like this? Why'd you do this to him?"

They tried to explain. They had done what they could to make him look presentable, a difficult job considering what had happened. They were earnest and, to their credit, calm.

I, however, was not calm. I was out of control. I had flipped a switch.

"I don't care!" I clasped the coffin, looking at my father, or what was once my father. "I don't understand why he's peach!"

Trey started yelling at me to calm down. I redirected my wrath toward him.

"How did you let them do this to him?" I howled. "What is wrong with you?"

"Ashley, you need to calm down!" Trey said.

I started screaming at the funeral people again.

Trey started in on Ann. "Why did let her get drunk?" he yelled at her.

"Trey, she's an adult woman." She quickly retorted. "If that is how she wants to handle it, that is how she's going to handle it."

"Please control her," he pleaded with Ann.

It was bedlam, like a black comedy gone amok. The others were stunned and gasping. I had saved the best for last.

I rushed to the edge of the coffin, lunged over the top, picked my father up and started to hug him, pulling him out of the coffin and screaming, "Daddy!"

The funeral people converged on me. The person in charge was frantic, trying to warn me that if I didn't stop, I might undo their delicate patchwork to hide my father's "head injury"— a funeral euphemism for somebody with their brains blown out—and that I was going to make a mess. So what? If that happened, why couldn't you fix him again? How hard could it be?

Still holding my father in my arms, I said that if she didn't leave me alone, I would sue her and the funeral home, and that she needed to "get the fuck away from me." I would have crawled in the coffin with him if I could have figured out how to do it.

Okay, fair enough, I had gone temporarily insane, in a manner of speaking.

But people failed to realize that a large piece of me died with my father. I had suffered bad stuff before, events that scarred me for life, but nothing like this. This was far, far worse than anything I'd had to handle in my twenty-five years. It was way more than what I endured as a result of my parents' divorce, what I suffered when molested as a minor, and the degradation of having sex for the first time with someone who treated me like shit. This was final, something I could not undo, that no one could undo. It couldn't be fixed with an apology. I couldn't kneel in a church pew, get solemn, and implore a higher power to make it all go away. There was no way out of this one. It was a forever pain that ripped up my insides.

There my father lay, in a long box, while everyone was trying to tell me I was wrong for doing what I was doing. It didn't feel wrong to hug my father. It didn't feel wrong to cry. It didn't feel wrong to dissemble. Nor would I have felt wrong to jump into the coffin and cozy up beside my father, which part of me yearned to do.

It should have been obvious that my father's death had traumatized me. Why wasn't everyone dealing with me on that level? All anyone seemed to care about was how to derail the train wreck I had become, to make sure I didn't trample on their shoes and heels and complicate things for them. No one, for example, suggested they clear the room to give me a few minutes alone with my father, not even the funeral parlor staff standing watch. Their go-to mentality was to wrap the poor thing in a straitjacket and shunt her aside.

I put my father down and stormed out of the room. My only regret was that I didn't get to witness the collective sigh of relief I am sure followed my footsteps out the door. The crazy woman was gone. Hallelujah.

Ann followed me out and I resumed my rant in her car, flailing about with my feet from the front passenger seat until I smashed the front windshield with a deftly placed front kick. Ann, bless her, was cool as a cucumber. She latched onto my legs and said with remarkable restraint, "You need to stop. You're either going to break your legs or something else in my car, and neither will be good."

I suspended the histrionics. Ann gave me a long and loving hug. She told me she had never seen me this upset or crazed. That made two of us.

I kept assuring her I would pay for the damage and she kept

assuring me that everything was okay. I knew I had crossed some lines and lost my shit. I was operating under a Molotov cocktail mixture of anger, sadness, and guilt. Anger at whoever did this to Dad and at my father for getting himself killed. Sadness at his loss and the emptiness I knew would be with me for a long time. Guilt for not making best use of time with my father and not being a better daughter. It was an incendiary blend of raw emotions and it made me crazy.

I added a few emotional years to my life that day. I had found forces inside I didn't know existed. Were they merely one person's grieving *in extremis* or was something more complex rising to the surface? I would have to wait to find out. For the time being, I had a funeral on my calendar in the morning.

7

I AWOKE ON THURSDAY, MAY 23, emotionally and physically depleted. I felt beat up, like a truck had rolled over me, back and forth a few times. My head ached and my neck was tight. My arms and legs felt numb. My heart felt like an anvil. I wanted to pull the covers over my head and stay underneath forever. I wanted this experience over.

I didn't know how I'd handle later. It didn't take me long to figure that out.

I had vodka remaining from the day before. I told myself that I couldn't face the burial sober. I needed to medicate. I found a glass and poured.

By the time Ann came over, I had made meaningful inroads toward right and proper burial day inebriation, Irish-wake style. Her smile when she entered my room signaled she smelled the evidence. She didn't comment. She didn't judge. She did, however, take a pass when I offered her a swig. It was, after all, not even 10 a.m. and she was driving. At least one of us retained good judgment.

I finished the booze and got as ready as I could to face the day. I took a deep breath and exhaled. I shook my head. The visual of putting my father into the earth disgusted me.

The service was scheduled for 10:30 a.m. We gathered our things and took that ever important final glance in the mirror to make sure we looked our feminine best. And off we went. We were headed first to the funeral parlor to join family members for the procession to The Church Alive, the site of the memorial service. The mission of The Church Alive, it bears noting, was to provide a haven for the "hurting, depressed, and frustrated." Throw open the doors, your most eligible penitent is on her way.

Once in the car, my mind went away, I don't know where. I locked into a daze the entire ride, staring into space silently. Ann left me to myself. She understood.

Ann was a constant godsend. She got me, always did. She embraced me on my terms, with love. She was my emotional bodyguard. Without her, I might have gone literally mad.

I had every intention that morning of flying under the radar at the funeral. The past two days had sapped me as I, no doubt, had done to a few others myself. Despite my feelings toward certain family members, I knew I had overstayed my welcome with some. It seemed fair that I spare them further emotional terrorism the day of the funeral.

To some extent, I have my father's youngest brother, Uncle Matt, to thank for my softened perspective. Earlier in the week he'd approached me sporting that "caring uncle" look. He put his hand on my shoulder and said, "We all grieve in our own way," and that I "should not feel bad" about how I chose to express what I was going through. I nodded, without comment. What I heard then was, "We know you are acting like madwoman, and that is okay. We forgive you."

It was a genuine gesture. Uncle Matt knew I was in a horrible place.

While I knew his words were meant for me, after they sunk in deeper, I could see they applied to the others as well. I knew that each one was suffering to varying degrees and I didn't own a monopoly on grief. Sure, our relationships were more complicated than that. But with some distance, with my uncle's kind hearted words staying with me, I could cut them some slack—not too much, mind you, but some. Doing so didn't compromise my feelings. It freed me to feel beyond my own pain.

So, as I approached the church steps, I committed to grieving in silence and allowing others to handle pain their way. I would try to be invisible among the other mourners.

I almost pulled it off.

I meandered down the center aisle of the church. Ann stayed close enough to keep a watchful eye on me. I expected my brother and mother to join me up front. As I gazed around the church, I noticed my dear brother with a small entourage around him, including his father-in-law, our pastor, and the pastor's son, all compassionate people helping my brother in time of need. Not to worry about me! I had vodka and Ann. All good here.

I looked up to see that someone had compiled a picture tribute to my father. I did a double-take. Déjà vu all over again. It didn't take much.

Someone had taken it upon themselves to arrange a pictorial display of my father without involving me. Maddening. But what I objected to, more than being left out again, was how gaudy and distasteful the damn thing looked. It didn't resemble in any way what I'd have done, nor did it appear to have a snowball's chance in hell of being what my father would have wanted. My father deserved much better. I know, I should have been grateful someone went to the trouble. But it didn't do Dad justice. It didn't do him right.

Was I overreacting? Had my spirit gotten so damaged I couldn't think straight? Fair questions. *Maybe,* I thought, *I should go with the flow.* Yes, now there's a novel concept, picking my spots. Remember what Uncle Matt told you? *We all grieve in our own ways.* I decided to keep my mouth shut, content to shake my head to myself as a silent form of protest.

Moments later, however, I detected two men setting up a video camera. Were they about to film the funeral? Are you fucking kidding me? I mean, holy shit, this wasn't a wedding. Why in the hell would anyone want to film a private funeral? I couldn't imagine the day when I would dust off the video of my dad's funeral to show my children—"Hey kids, look at the grandfather you never met; I know you can't see him, but isn't it a pretty box?"—or friends at a dinner party like people do with vacation footage—"Hey everyone, how about, after dessert, we watch Dad's funeral? Wait until you see the picture collage of my father someone put together!"

Was it me? Do people do such things? Was it normal?

The audacity thoroughly offended me. I walked up to two filmmakers and said, "No way, boys" in a loud tone that didn't inspire negotiation. To remove the doubt from their incredulous looks, I followed with, "And, gentlemen, if you don't take the camera down immediately, I'll be more than happy to do it for you."

The two poor guys stumbled backwards, stunned. They never banked on resistance from a mad and ferocious woman. They tried to explain that Trey gave them permission. I countered that I was Carter Elliott's daughter, and if they didn't remove the cameras, I'd resort to self-help. They complied.

I often have wondered whether they skulked away to a different location and filmed anyway, and that somewhere, in someone's garage or attic, buried in a storage box with other unused times long forgotten, lies a video of Dad's funeral. Perish the thought.

The rest of the memorial is a blur, thankfully, save one part. I remember they played "Amazing Grace," my father's favorite hymn. It was fitting, of course but, as I listened, the setting managed to squeeze the sweetness out of that beautiful song. For me, "Amazing Grace" will perpetually be associated with death and the worst days of my life.

As the curtain came down on the memorial and others mulled around and said to each whatever people tend to say in those situations, I didn't linger. I made a beeline to the hearse that would transport me to the Crestlawn Memorial Park for the burial service. I sat there alone until we were ready to go, my head resting on the back of the seat, my eyes closed, counting grueling seconds until the finale.

After a short while, my mother, my father's other ex-wife Sara, and my father's current girlfriend Christie, slipped into the limousine. How perfect was that? The three loves of my father's life, during different periods, joined at the hip in a hearse en route to his burial! I stifled the escalating urge to erupt in hysterics. I smiled to myself, knowing that wherever my father's spirit was, he was smiling ear to ear with a thumbs up to the sky. He couldn't have scripted it better.

No one spoke the whole way. We each stayed within ourselves. What could we possibly talk about? Forget about me, what could the three objects of my dad's romantic affection possibly say to each other? "You know, I just love that dress." "Now, pray tell, where did you get those darling earrings?" "And that perfume! Do I detect white-amber, musk, and vanilla?"

It's amazing how much entertainment can be culled from silence and a little imagination during a ride to a cemetery.

I zoned during the burial service. I didn't hear what was said, relegating spoken words to a background hum, painfully aware of what was coming. When they lowered the coffin, I cried softly to myself, head down. I kept reminding myself that my father would have wanted me to be strong and stoic. I did my best as Daddy's little girl. I kept drawing on him.

I didn't stir when everyone moved to their cars. I watched them all go, leaving me alone at the grave site. After a while, the father of my sister-in-law, Trey's wife, returned to retrieve me. I joined the romance trio in the limo to return to the church for food and socializing, a ritual I dreaded like the plague. Again, on the return trip, no one spoke.

When we arrived, everyone was sitting and standing around, eating fried chicken, talking up storms, and reliving memories. I couldn't get up for post-funeral repartée. I kept reverting to the visual of the corpse and peach lipstick and the dumping of the overpriced coffin into the overpriced dirt. Funeral customs seemed barbaric and grotesque. There had to be a better way.

I saw my former stepmother Sara, my dad's second wife, sitting alone. Sara and I had made no bones about not liking each other. And at that point in my life, I lacked the social skills to converse seamlessly with a person I did not like. But something compelled me to sit with her. I mumbled something about needing to apologize. She gave me a confused look.

I apologized for taking down all her pictures in the house and stepping on them when I found out she and Dad were engaged. I apologized for throwing her clothes out of my mother's closet. I apologized for calling her a bitch. An apology trifecta.

I was rather proud of myself for making the effort. A part of me meant what I said. Another part wasn't quite sure. I was still a few sheets to the wind. Maybe "I hate you" might have been more appropriate, more candid. But calling up a litany of regrets made me feel good.

Sara looked at me, first incredulously, and then as if she were watching paint dry. *Say something Sara*, I thought. *Give me something, please. I'm hanging on a limb here.*

Nothing. Not a word. She turned her head away, adult-speak for "get away from me." Beautiful. Such a sweetheart. I should have opted for "I hate you."

I knew it was time to leave.

I grabbed Ann and said we needed to return to the cemetery. I had earlier asked her to buy a bottle of Crown Royal, my father's booze of choice, and a can of Coke. My father like to blend Crown Royal and Coca-Cola to make what he called milkshakes, especially before going out on the town. I told Ann, "We're going to have some milkshakes as the last hurrah."

The three of us, meaning Ann, the beverages and I, made our way back to the cemetery to honor my father. When we arrived, we noticed flowers sprawled sloppily on the gravesite, as if tossed as an afterthought. We rearranged them. They now looked great.

Ann and I sat and talked for about an hour, taking sips of the milkshakes, always toasting my father. It was the first time the entire week I felt some calm. I had finally gotten the quiet time with my father I needed, my first opportunity to connect with his spirit unimpeded by family dynamics and public rituals.

Ann and I talked about family. We talked about my father and his colorful life and that, no matter what people might say about him— and we were soon to hear plenty once the criminal investigation got in full swing—he had lived his way with an unbridled spirit. He didn't half-ass anything. He was all-in, and sometimes to a fault.

My father, more than anything, was his own man. I admired him for that.

I also laughed about how over the top I had been the past few days.

When I'd had enough, I emptied what was left in the Crown Royal bottle onto the burial plot, a last drink for my dad. I grabbed a bunch of dirt from the spot and jammed it into the bottle as an enduring monument. I have the dirt-filled bottle to this day.

That night, I let it all hang loose. We hit a bar, and I drank and drank and snorted cocaine and meth, whatever was available. As if it were planned, a steady stream of people who knew my father visited me to share their story. One would come over, tell their tale, and leave, clearing the way for the next visitor. It was the flip side of the wedding congratulations line, except no one came bearing envelopes full of cash, Italian-style. I didn't want to hear the stories but politely listened. It was torturous.

Predictably, though, I eventually lost it.

One storyteller was a Marine, soon to be deployed in Afghanistan. Maybe, I thought, I should hook him up with Dick Conte. How about that for a novel idea?

By that time of the night, unfortunately for the young Marine, I had my fill of drunks wanting to pay homage to my father. I had been reduced to the lowest common denominator of social interaction and treated him accordingly. In other words, I was a bitch to him. I was drunk and sick, as his earnest voice pounded the shit out of me. I felt trapped in an echo chamber and wanted to scream. Instead,

I think I told him to "Shut the fuck up" at some point. Next thing I knew I was in the bathroom vomiting, Ann holding my hair and me presiding over a disgusting pile of the day's ingestions.

I wanted to join my father in death, do anything to make myself numb, anything to take the hurt away. I needed to go to the hospital, but went home instead.

Ann dropped me off at the Howard Johnson's that night. I struggled to fall asleep. I couldn't free my mind of the cold reality I faced, lying in the darkness of the hotel room. Dad's not coming back. He was dead. He had vanished for eternity.

I'll never again see his beautiful blue eyes. I'll never again hear his half-man, half-child Southern voice and his raucous laugh that filled rooms. I'll never again see him hold court as the center of attention, playing a larger-than-life role as only he could. I'll never again see him drink so much to act the fool, trying to one-up his youthful entourage.

He'll no longer give me shit or tell me what to do, which suddenly I missed and wanted.

Worse, our unfinished business as a father and daughter will forever remain unfinished. He'll get no more chances to treat me as Daddy's little girl, or be the sweet and thoughtful mentor I knew deep down he would eventually become for me.

I, in turn, will not have the chance to mature with him so that I can openly embrace all his traits, including flaws and excesses, while he did the same for me.

I'll be denied the chance to watch him grow older and soften the way people can over time, seeing the world through a wiser lens. I won't ever see him be a loving and doting grandfather to my children.

I'll never get to hug him whenever the impulse strikes, to hold him tight, and tell him what I now felt I didn't tell him enough: "I love you, Daddy."

We loved each other, didn't we? I was still a good daughter to him, wasn't I? And, despite all the vitriol I leveled at him, he was a good father to me, wasn't he?

I'm never going to—never—see him again.

PART II

8

THE CONWAY POLICE DEPARTMENT, FBI, and Arkansas State Police, working in concert, began to identify potential witnesses, inspect financial, phone, and other records, give Miranda warnings, issue polygraph tests, conduct interviews, and explore motives and suspects. As they did, a timeline of the days leading to the twin murders emerged. Here is some of what the investigative files show.

WEDNESDAY, MAY 15, 2002

During the afternoon, my father and Timmy Wayne hit the bar at the Hardscrabble Country Club in Fort Smith, Arkansas. There they met two married women in their twenties who were coming off a tennis match. The four shared drinks and spirited banter in plain view. The rumor mill was greased lightning. It didn't take long for gossip to spread about angry husbands bristling at Dad's flirtatious style.

That night, my father visited the Centennial Valley Country Club with David Clark, a close friend and local prosecutor, to listen to a Dave Matthews cover band. As they eased into the night, a dude named Eddie ambled past their table and flashed my father a snarly look. During the previous month or so, my father had complained to

Clark that this guy didn't like my dad for reasons he couldn't figure out. Dad told Clark that one of these days, he would "whip Eddie's ass" and "clean the floor with him."

That night, Eddie crept up close to my father, and without provocation, said something nasty.

My father shrugged, "Why don't you like me?"

The guy said, "You're a smartass and an asshole."

It got heated, and someone from the club came over and ushered Eddie away. My dad was perplexed. "I don't know why that son-of-a-bitch doesn't like me, but he doesn't like me, and if he wants to start something, I'll finish it."

THURSDAY, MAY 16, 2002

During the afternoon of May 16, Dad had received a phone call that got heated quickly. At one point, my father told the caller, "You better not bring your sorry ass over here, that's not anything you want to be doing." A witness said he'd "never seen Carter that upset."

That night, my father and Timmy Wayne spent time at Cajun's Wharf in Little Rock with several other friends, including David Clark, and "a bunch of girls." Someone commented that my father was not his usual outgoing self, "hadn't acted like himself" for the past few weeks, and seemed "worried about something." A Detco employee added that my father "was in some kind of trouble." In the weeks before, my father had several conversations with someone about becoming his bodyguard.

FRIDAY, MAY 17, 2020

The next day, my father and Timmy Wayne continued working on the Shady Valley house getting the deck and pool ready for a party my father planned to host on Sunday in the early evening. They had spent most days that week getting the place in party shape.

Christie Jameson spent most of the day indoors with her sister, cooking for a wedding shower scheduled for the next day in Brinkley, Tennessee, where her mother lived. The two left around 5:30 p.m. to return to Memphis.

Before going out for the night, my father received a call from an unidentified male caller, who left this message: "Hey, dude, I just got some information on Danny Hall up there. When you get a chance, give me a call. Adam called and told me he said he thinks he has closed the doors."

My father and Timmy Wayne decided to go the West End Tavern in Little Rock that night, arriving at about 10:00 p.m. It didn't take long for them to hook up with three women, Alexis Cantrell, Paulina Turner and Charlotte Andrews. Turner and Andrews were sisters and Cantrell was married. My father reputedly enticed the three women into performing an abbreviated amateur audition for a strip club act.

At midnight, David Clark showed up at the West End Tavern to meet another friend and found my dad and Timmy Wayne at the front door of the club, about to leave with the three women. They told Clark they were off to a Taco Bell and, after a few exchanges, went separate ways. After searching the club and not seeing his friend, Clark left to find the group at the nearest Taco Bell.

About 12:30 a.m., Clark found the five of them at the Taco Bell sitting in one car in the drive-thru takeout line. Clark parked his car and got into the other car with them. The women got food and ate, and the group of six debated what to do with the rest of the evening. Timmy Wayne said he was going to his girlfriend's house to crash, taking my father's Lexus. David Clark said he'd drive my father home. Timmy Wayne got phone numbers from the women to call them the next day.

At 1:30, en route their separate ways, the three men reconsidered their exit strategy and decided to hit the Electric Cowboy night club in Little Rock. While there, my father ran into a woman named Crystal for whom he apparently had a longstanding infatuation. He wound up spending the rest of the evening flirting with her, interrupted only by a cell phone conversation he had with his girlfriend, Christie, around 1:50 in the morning

They stayed at the Electric Cowboy until it closed at 5:00 a.m. Crystal tried to lure my father to a party in West Little Rock. Clark talked him out of it, concerned about a drug scene at the party. They elected to call it a night as the sun began to rise.

At 6:00 a.m., Clark got my father home. Dad was so drunk he stumbled and fell in his driveway. Clark waited until my father made it safely inside before going home.

Timmy Wayne headed to his girlfriend's place. When she awoke the next morning about six hours later, he was gone. She reported that Timmy Wayne had "been acting different" recently.

SATURDAY, MAY 18, 2002

Sometime before 9:00 a.m., Timmy Wayne, on limited sleep, arrived at Shady Valley and made the first of many calls to the three women from the night before to invite them to hang out at the house pool. They declined the invitation.

Around the same time, Mike Kountze, a business partner of my father, invited Dad to breakfast at Stoby's Restaurant in Conway. Timmy Wayne and my father arrived at Stoby's at 9:30, joining Kountze, his girlfriend Brandi Thaden and a longstanding friend, Jake Beals. My father arrived looking disheveled.

During the breakfast, the others jokingly gave my father shit about his penchant for pissing off boyfriends and husbands. My dad admitted he had annoyed some guys the night before at Electric Cowboy Club by flirting with their girlfriends. He also mentioned he had incurred the ire of a married man by making the moves on the guy's mistress.

The breakfast ended around 10:30, and on the way home, my father took a call from Christie Jameson, who was back in Memphis.

They discussed the upcoming pool party and Christie's plans that day to go to Brinkley, Tennessee for the wedding shower. My father and Timmy Wayne arrived at Shady Valley at about 10:45.

Shortly thereafter, around 11:00, David Clark arrived at Shady Valley to borrow a Detco power washer my father promised he could use to clean his deck. My father recommended that Clark take his brown Chevrolet truck to transport the washer rather than trying to fit the thing into his Jeep.

At about 11:45, my father's housekeeper, Mary Beck, arrived to clean the house. As she did, Clark was walking out the front door and my father and Timmy Wayne were in the garage loading the power washer into the brown truck. The three men then left in two cars, Clark driving the truck and my father and Timmy Wayne in Dad's Lexus. Clark left his Jeep at Shady Valley. My father and Timmy Wayne followed Clark home to help unload the power washer before returning home.

On his return, Timmy Wayne again attempted to entice the three women from the previous night to come over. They were having lunch at Chili's Grill and Bar in Conway with plans to go shopping afterward, and again declined. They promised to call later.

Sometime around noon, Christie Jameson and my father spoke again. He was back in bed. They chatted for a few minutes.

At 2:00 p.m., Tess Arnold, another woman with whom my father had spent time, arrived at Shady Valley. Tess found my father in his bed upstairs wearing the clothes he'd worn the night before. At some point, while cleaning, Mary noticed my father with his shirt off and Tess giving him a back rub. When Tess saw Mary, she called out, "Tell Carter to let me go." My father insisted Tess stay, but she said she had to leave. As she walked down the stairs, Timmy Wayne blurted out, "Why don't you give Carter some action before you leave?" Tess paid Timmy Wayne no mind and left, after which my father asked Mary, "Why did you let that crazy woman in my house?"

At 2:45 p.m., Alan Duke and his son arrived at Shady Valley to grab the brown truck to transport garden plants and related items they were planning to buy. Duke went upstairs and found my father in his bedroom, asleep, and left him undisturbed.

Ten minutes later, at 2:55, Pete Ballinger, a friend of Dad's, showed up looking for my dad who apparently, along with my uncles Matt (aka David) and Rusty, was supposed to meet Ballinger earlier at the family lake house in Choctaw. None of them showed up. Duke told Ballinger my father was upstairs sleeping. Ballinger left.

Mary left Shady Valley at 3:15. She thought my father was either drunk or drugged that day. The entire vibe at the house made her uncomfortable. She couldn't wait to leave.

At about 4:30, Timmy Wayne called the three women again to come over, but they had dinner plans. Timmy Wayne said he'd catch them later at the West End Tavern. During the call, Kountze and Thaden from breakfast arrived to hang out by the pool with Timmy Wayne and my father.

About the same time, Alan Duke called Clark about using the brown truck. Clark told Duke he could come get the truck but he needed it back to return the power washer.

At around 5:30, my father and Christie Jameson talked again by cell phone.

Kountze and Thaden left Shady Valley at 6:00.

At 6:49, my father called his brother Rusty and didn't reach him.

At 7:19, my father called the local Conway hospital, where his business partner, J.T. Jones, a chronic diabetic, was in ICU following a toe amputation. Dad wanted to see if it was okay to come by for a visit. He didn't reach him. Fifteen minutes later, at 7:34, my father spoke to J.T.'s wife, Susan, who gave him the green light to visit. My father and Timmy Wayne visited J.T. shortly thereafter.

At 8:02, my father called my brother's wife. They spoke briefly.

At 8:23, my father tried unsuccessfully to contact Alan Duke. Earlier that week, my father had told Duke that if something happened to him, Duke needed to know what to do. Duke was then suffering from a serious stomach condition and asked my father to agree to reciprocate. A standing tongue-in-cheek joke, perhaps not so funny to Duke, was that if Duke died, my father would wind up with his wife, Kimberly.

Following the missed call to Duke, my father and Timmy Wayne went to the local Taco Bell for takeout dinner. The time stamp on the Taco Bell receipt read 8:52 p.m.

It takes less than five minutes to get from the Taco Bell on Prince Street in Conway to my father's house. Two neighbors spotted Dad's Lexus in the circle drive outside his house at about 9:00. My father never parked in the circle drive outside the house, so it seemed that someone else, likely Timmy Wayne, had driven the car.

Alexis Cantrell, one of the three women from the night before, called Timmy Wayne again between 10:00 and 10:30 from the West End but didn't reach him. The women left a joint voicemail message for Timmy Wayne and my father, letting them know they planned to leave the West End and continue their night out at the Electric Cowboy. They urged the men to join them.

Sometime between 10:00 and 11:00, Christie and my father talked briefly on the phone while she was with a friend at Alfred's on Beale Street in Memphis. My father told her that he and Timmy Wayne and had decided to stay home and watch a movie—unheard of for them on a Saturday night.

At 11:29, Christie called my father again but got no answer. She left a message on his voicemail, that she and her friend Nikki would be at the Rhinestone Cowboy riding the bull, and they'd wait for him to come. "Get your ass over here for some motherfucking fun. We want Timmy Wayne to be there, too."

She called again at 12:01 a.m. and left another voicemail message: "Hi! In case you forgot my name, this is Doctor Christie Elliott. . . . You need to call my cell phone. . . . So, I mean, you know, call your wife."

She called again five minutes later, at 12:06, and didn't leave a message, and again at 1:16, leaving this message: "Hello. You know this is 1:15; it is your wife, in case you forgot my name. You know [to] call my phone. Bye."

SUNDAY, MAY 19, 2002

The next morning at 10:05, Christie called my dad and left this message: "I just forgot you're in church. We just now woke up, still lying in bed . . . When you get out of church, call me, goodbye."

At 12:05 p.m., Christie called Jake Beals and left a voicemail message. She told Beals that my father was in a bad mood and apparently didn't want to see her, and he asked Beals to check on him. Beals didn't follow up.

At 12:49, Christie tried my father again, leaving this message: "I thought you were in church, but you should be out of church by now. I haven't heard back from you, so please call me, I'm worried, bye."

While watching a Major League Baseball game in the early afternoon, David Clark received a page from Christie that he please call her. Christie wanted to know what was up with my father not returning her calls, but Clark didn't call her.

At 1:05 p.m., Christie called my father again. She and her friend Nikki were scheduled to be at Shady Valley after 6 that evening for the pool party at Dad's house. The two women were still in Memphis and preparing to drive to Conway, and Christie wanted to make sure the party was still on the social agenda, increasingly uncertain because of the lack of responses to her calls. She left this voicemail message: "Carter, why don't you miss me? I do not understand. Good-bye."

Less than an hour later, at 1:56, she called and left this message: "Guess what, it's still me. I haven't heard from you. Bye."

At 3:03, Christie called again, leaving this message: "Okay, I just want you to know, its 3:05, Nikki and I are leaving Memphis, and you're getting a divorce, bye." The women began the drive from Memphis to Conway.

At around 6:00, as Christie and Nikki neared Conway, Christie made repeated unanswered calls to my father, thinking he had decided to do something else without telling her. She called every phone number she had. She was getting angry.

At about 6:30, Christie and Nikki arrived at the Shady Valley house. Christie noticed David Clark's Jeep outside and assumed that Timmy Wayne, Clark, and my father were out back at the swimming pool. They walked around the back of the house and peeked over the fence, seeing no one. They tried to enter the home through the garage door. It was locked. They returned to the front door. It was unlocked.

Christie opened the door gently and they stepped inside. The first thing Christie noticed was two bodies on the floor, face down, drenched in blood—one in the foyer and the other nearby in the living room. The women both ran outside, screaming for help, and found two men in a yard next door working on a car. They yelled for them to call 911.

At 6:44 p.m., when the Conway Police Department arrived, the front door was flung wide open, and on the front step before the entrance was a partially eaten candy bar in a wrapper. They secured the area, determined that the persons inside were dead, and called for legal and medical personnel, including the office of the local prosecutor, the fire department (to confirm the men inside were deceased), and the coroner's office (to do what medical examiners do).

My brother, Trey, got word that something was amiss at my father's place, but the information was fuzzy. He was told police were arriving at the property. He called my dad's brother, Uncle Matt, and told him, "I think something is wrong with my dad." He added that he had been told, "The next-door neighbor is crying, and they are starting to rope something off." Uncle Matt went immediately to pick up Trey and his wife, a five-minute drive. As the three drove around the corner toward the house, they could hear the scratchy cackle of police radios and could see a cadre of police vehicles, flashing lights, a gathering crowd, and fire trucks.

Uncle Matt said, "Trey, this is not going to be good."

They got out of the car and ran toward the house. Someone from the Conway PD told them my father had been shot and was dead. The police asked Trey and Uncle Matt about the cars outside, thinking the other victim was local prosecutor, David Clark. When the police described the second victim, Uncle Matt said, "That would be Timmy Wayne."

Uncle Matt called his brother Rusty to let him know. He also asked him to call their mother and me.

While this was happening, David Clark got a call from someone asking if he knew what was happening at Carter Elliott's house. He didn't, but realized he needed to go there. He arrived shortly after 7:00 p.m.. After talking to Conway police officers, he was asked to enter the residence to formally identify the bodies. He agreed, went inside, and identified the men as my father and Timmy Wayne.

At 10:15 the local FBI arrived. After getting briefed by Sgt. Jim Barrett of the Conway PD and the ERT (Emergency Response Team), the FBI took official control of the crime scene.

For the next several hours, the FBI took photos and swabs from various bloodstains, collected what evidence they could find, directed certain sketches to be made, examined the bodies, and dusted for fingerprints.

The police found nothing missing from the residence and in fact found a "large sum of money" on top of a bible in my father's bedroom. Later, however, word circulated that a black bag my father used for carrying cash was missing. At first, the amount presumed in the black bag was $10,000. Later, it became $100,000, raising eyebrows. In addition, two diamonds that supposedly were in a Detco coffee cup also turned up missing.

MONDAY, MAY 20, 2002

Shortly after 2:00 a.m., the coroner removed the bodies.

At 4:45, FBI officials returned control of the crime scene to the Conway Police Department. A few hours later, Conway PD "released" the property to the family.

At 11:49, ServiceMasters in North Little Rock received a call from someone who identified himself as Alan Duke. The caller was upset, explaining there had been a murder, and he needed a trauma cleanup done in thirty minutes. ServiceMasters said that wasn't practical, which upset the caller (presumably Duke), who insisted on the cleanup getting done "immediately."

Jeff Beebe of ServiceMasters arrived to do the job. Duke gave Beebe precise instructions on which parts of the home he wanted scrubbed. After Beebe was done, Duke asked him to remove all remaining crime scene tape. Beebe declined. Duke then asked Beebe to deep-six three magazines that had fingerprint dust on them. Beebe obliged.

As the week unfolded, the Conway PD, Arkansas State Police, and FBI geared up for a full-scale coordinated criminal investigation. The initial official word was, they had "no suspects" and "no motive" and a crime scene "unlike any" they had seen before. Where the investigation was headed was anyone's guess.

9

INVESTIGATORS LEARNED FAST THAT MY father left a wide swath over the course of his brief life. He was an extrovert by nature, to a fault some would add, engaging a diverse group of acquaintances beyond his family and inner circle of running buddies. Among his many relationships and associations, he counted gambling and business partners, church congregation members, people down and out needing a lift or second chance, employees, country club members and staff, local civil servants, an array of folks who served the public in bars, nightclubs and restaurants, and, of course, an uninterrupted parade of young ladies he lusted over.

The more people the investigators interviewed, the more the witness list propagated, like the biblical loaves and fishes. Most everybody had at least one Carter Elliott story to tell, many more than one, and all eager to tell them, some perhaps too eager. There were those, too, and not a few, who weren't shy about teeing up unsolicited seat-of-the-pants whodunit opinions.

Day by day, investigators widened the playing field, sniffing out all sorts of leads, some promising, many speculative, and others, it seemed, ginned up. Four weeks into it, they boasted an impressive list of theories and potential suspects. Here's a glimpse of the early returns based on a review of the records obtained using public records request procedures.

THE DRUG DEALER HIT

Drugs was an early focus. My father's penchant for toting thousands of dollars in cash when out on the town, and the appearance of a professional hit, naturally urged in that direction.

Most everyone acknowledged, though, that my father didn't dabble in drugs. He lived hard and sometimes drank to excess. But his lifestyle didn't include pharmaceuticals, marijuana, or other recreational enhancers. On the contrary, people were emphatic that my father "hated drug use" and went the extra mile to help those with drug problems. That he would be involved in drug dealing was counterintuitive.

One Detco employee, however, suggested my dad had a cocaine habit.

"A coke person knows a coke person. [Carter's] swings and moods, nobody has energy in the world like that, especially at seven o'clock in the morning. His highs and lows every other minute were astronomical. A man at forty-eight years old cannot walk with energy fourteen hours straight like that."

My mother told investigators that, in her view, the mood swings and high energy were the product of a manic-depressive personality, a dynamic which Trey and I knew all too well. My dad swung on an emotional pendulum second to none.

Besides, even if true, putting cocaine up your nose to jumpstart the day is a far cry from being immersed in drug dealing on a scale to get you killed. More was needed for that theory to have legs. It turns out, there was.

The drug dealer motive became more than a theory when a frantic Alan Duke visited the Shady Valley house unexpectedly, two weeks after the murders. My mother and I were cleaning when Duke tried to enter the locked front door. He pounded on the door with agitation. My mom turned to me and said, loud enough for him to hear, "Do you want me to open [the door]?" Duke beat me to the answer: "Yes, open it!" I let him in.

He was nervous. He babbled on and on about a missing "black bag." He wanted to search for it in one of the cars, the white Mercedes, exclaiming the bag held $100,000 in cash. He also wanted to find some missing diamonds, which he said my father stored in a Detco plastic cup. We had no clue about either.

We searched the car and found nothing, and he left.

I shared this little episode with the police. Aspects of the case that law enforcement might have earlier dismissed as fanciful now exhibited new meaning. For example, one witness told the Arkansas State Police: "Carter Elliott was in every kind of business. I mean everything. If you understand what I mean." Another told the FBI he knew someone who knew "who pulled the trigger, and that it wasn't important, the two men that were killed were just dopers anyway . . . . The older man who was killed was the leader of the drug operation, and the younger man who was killed was the one who bought and distributed the drugs."

Did my father and Timmy Wayne have a secret life? Was my father's anti-drugs campaign a front?

Then, someone claimed that an unidentified party used the Detco facility to "mix and cook" drugs at the behest of my father, a narrative that stole a page from the *Breaking Bad* TV series. According to this new story, those involved used an interstate trucking company to move illicit product through a Mexican contact in California, and that a former Detco employee was central to the operation.

The FBI interviewed the former Detco employee and read him standard Miranda rights. He agreed to answer questions without counsel present and take a polygraph test. Among the questions put to him were, "Did you take part in this shooting?" and "Do you know who was involved with this shooting?" He answered no to both.

The polygraph finding was that "the psychological responses noted on this subject's polygraph charts are in such a pattern indicating that the charts are inconclusive," leaving his truthfulness unresolved.

THE JEALOUS HUSBAND

Investigators looked at whether Alan Duke may have directed the killings, presumably because he could no longer tolerate how my father and Duke's wife, Kimberly, carried on. While my father and Alan Duke were good friends and business partners, they had their sideways moments. One person described their relationship as "love-hate."

Kimberly Duke acknowledged that she and my father "loved each other and had a close relationship." She joked "about her ending up with Carter in the future." And while they "talked about [having an affair] from time to time," Kimberly Duke insisted they never took the plunge. My father also had denied any affair.

At least two witnesses, however, claimed they "were having an affair." One also claimed she once saw them at a social event pressed up against each other, nose to nose, and when Alan Duke spotted them, he sternly told my father to "let go of" his wife. Another person claimed that same night they saw my father "reach under Kimberly's skirt." The next day, reportedly, Alan Duke was furious.

My father told me that Kimberly pressed him to have an affair because of a void in her sexual relationship with her husband. Dad said he declined. Alan Duke was his friend and he couldn't do that to him. Kimberly Duke said that the pressure for an affair originated with my father, and it was she, not Dad, who resisted advances.

Whatever the truth, Duke had noticed their not-so-secret sexual energy. He'd confronted them whenever the two were away together for unaccounted hours, and he worried that if he died, my father "would marry his wife . . . and move into" his house. In characteristic style, my father poked, "Your wife loves me more than she does you. Your kids love me."

It came to a head apparently when Alan Duke received an anonymous letter accusing Kimberly and my father of the affair. He was "distraught" and confronted them. They denied the affair and accused him of sending the letter himself to stir up shit.

People were starting to talk. "Alan Duke hated Carter because Carter was having an affair with Alan's wife." It got to the point where my father wouldn't visit Kimberly at her home unless her husband was present.

An interesting twist to the purported love triangle arose when both Dukes pushed investigators to look at Christie Jameson "as a suspect." Both labelled Christie a "gold-digger" who wanted to grab what money and jewelry she could find at Shady Valley. David Clark stoked the fire, urging prosecutors take a hard look at Christie: "Greed is a powerful tool." Clark was "confident Christie knew all about the" black bag with the missing cash and the diamonds.

Why were these people so intent on focusing investigators on Christie Jameson? Were they trying to direct attention away from Alan Duke? And what was up the with emergency cleanup of Shady Valley that Duke had arranged the morning of May 20, on the heels of the initial law enforcement inspection of the home? Was it designed to remove residual evidence once the police and FBI had swept through? What was the urgency?

Someone who knew my father well said that Dad "loved Kimberly to death." Were those ominous words?

THE ANGRY BOYFRIEND OR HUSBAND

More than one person suggested the killings may have come at the hands of an angry boyfriend or husband who was a stranger to my father. My father had raised the temperature of more than a few men by putting the moves on their ladies. One notable example occurred at the Centennial Country Club one evening when he repeatedly told a woman over a two-hour period that she should be better off with him than with the man seated next to her. Knowing my father, he thought he was being playful, but I'm betting the subjects of his standup routine saw it differently.

The investigative challenge was to match the scintillating theory with a specific person. Who might go to such lengths? Had any of the insulted men made threats? Did any have a history of violence? Did any own firearms?

A possible lead occurred when a retired El Dorado detective received a phone call from a woman claiming information about the murders. She said that her daughter and my father were having an affair at the time of the homicides, and she suspected her son-in-law. She confronted her daughter about the affair and her daughter responded with a question, whether it "was possible to be in love with two people." The murders happened two days later.

Another witness suggested that investigators take a look at a man in a relationship with a local twenty-six-year-old woman. My father had devoted a fair amount of attention to her to help her get on track with her life. He gave her a job and urged her to be self-supportive and live on her own. The attention apparently infuriated the boyfriend, who, it was said, owned guns he like to brandish and had a history of threatening people over women.

THE UNPAID GAMBLING DEBT

When investigators learned my father often gambled, regularly carried around gobs of cash, and had his jaw broken by a bookie in the recent past, the gambling debt theory inched toward the front of the line.

The threshold question was whether the gambling was high stakes enough to provoke a mob-style hit for an overdue debt. One witness offered that my father "always operated in the gray area," was "always robbing Peter to pay Paul," and "wanted people to think he had a lot of money." The implication was that there was a pattern of overextending and coming up short with the wrong people at the wrong time, like the lead character in the film, *Uncut Gems*.

The evidence fluctuated about how deep into the gambling pool my father had jumped. Some described small town poker games in local clubs with stakes no higher than $1,000 or $2,000. Others painted a more grandiose backdrop where my father gambled "really big," tossing around numbers as high as $100,000.

My mother put this spin on it to investigators: "Knowing him, he just got in over his head. I think somebody hired somebody to do it because he didn't pay them, or they didn't pay him, or he knew something he shouldn't have known."

THE REAL ESTATE PROJECT

Investigators spent considerable time looking at a real estate development project called Magnolia in Eagle Creek, Arkansas, and in particular Grayson Ramsey, who arranged the initial four-person investor group. My father acquired a piece of the action from an initial investor and, before long, problems arose between Dad and Ramsey.

My father once complained that Ramsey owed him $50,000 for monies loaned or guaranteed. He also complained that Ramsey finagled him out of a significant profit from the sale of certain lots. My understanding is that Ramsey vehemently denied having breached any legal duty to my father. At some point, my dad's attorney placed a lien on the property. My father also reportedly conferred with David Clark about whether Ramsey may have committed a fraud serious enough to land him in jail. His dealings with Ramsey inspired Dad to coin the refrain, "You've never been rodded until you've been Ramsrodded."

Ramsey also denied any wrongdoing in connection with the murders. He told investigators he had "no idea what could have happened to" my father and Timmy Wayne, and if anyone said he was involved in the shooting, they "would be a liar." He took a polygraph test that included questions like, if he "took part in the shooting," whether he was "involved in any way," and if he knew anyone "who was involved in the shooting." His denials were deemed "essentially truthful."

THE DISGRUNTLED EMPLOYEE

Two weeks before the twin homicides at Shady Valley, my father fired an employee who someone at Detco described as "a bad person," "gang banger," and "walking devil." The fired man evidently had a rap sheet and history of drug use.

Investigators learned that before the employee lost his job, he reportedly said, "If that motherfucker ever fires me, I have people in Florida that are professional. We tie them up, we'd slit their throats, we'd take a silencer to their head." He crowed at Detco that he had killed before.

The day of his firing the employee had a heated swearing match with my Uncle Matt and, when leaving Detco that day, told someone he "had an eight-ball of cocaine on him."

The results of the employee's polygraph test, which probed knowledge about the murders, were "inconclusive."

THE MOB

Several persons interviewed suggested the FBI take a look at mob involvement. The circumstances concerned Share Corporation, which someone said they thought the mob owned, although to my knowledge that was never substantiated.

As his attorney told it, my father "had a lot to do with Share going out of business." After he founded Detco, my father began to hire employees from Share, a competitor, and over time grabbed business away, expanding Detco's market share. Share eventually collapsed.

Even though the Share and Detco competition occurred in the 1980s and 90s, my father's attorney theorized that the owners of Share may have been waiting for the right time to get even. But the counter argument was that the mob's calling card doesn't typically include delayed revenge. As one law enforcement official observed, when the mob is unhappy, they don't dilly-dally. They act quickly and decisively. In all events, based on a review of the files, no one connected at Share was ever considered a person of interest or a suspect.

THE BEAUTY PAGEANT

Christie Jameson had beauty pageant aspirations. A previous Miss Arkansas Teen USA winner, she'd had a few unsuccessful runs at Miss Arkansas USA before concluding she needed to look elsewhere for pageant glory. She set her sights on Miss Tennessee USA.

Competing in Tennessee pageants, however, required residency. My father stepped up to help. He first set her up with a place to live in Memphis, and she won the Miss Memphis contest. She then set her eyes on Miss Tennessee USA, a crown that would clear the way to compete in the Miss USA contest. As rumors had it, my father greased palms with promises of more rewards if Christie won the crown.

Pageant officials concluded that Christie was a resident of Arkansas and her Memphis address a ruse and thus disqualified her. Reportedly incensed, my father refused to pay what he'd promised. Whether that was true, or how at risk he found himself, wasn't clear. And no names emerged from the investigative files. Other than speculation, nothing suggested that any pageant official with their hand still out would use a professional hit as a form of debt collection. But the theory sounded captivating.

THE HUMILIATED EMPLOYEE

Not surprisingly, investigators had sustained interest in relationships at Detco, my father's company. They wanted to know whether one employee (Joey Spencer), with whom I understand my father experienced difficulties, might have had reason to kill my father.

It was reported that Spencer hated how my father bossed him around at Detco. One person told investigators that Spencer "despised" my father "for having to work in a hot warehouse and having to ask" him for things.

A Detco employee described Spencer as a drug user, and said my father had surreptitiously taken a strand of his hair to test for cocaine. My father confided with office personnel that he thought Spencer might steal from him, and suspected Spencer peddled Detco chemicals on the black market.

Despite the innuendo, this became another dead end.

THE DENIED EX-WIFE

My mother didn't escape scrutiny.

Contrary to what I had thought before my father died—or convinced myself to believe—Dad evidently didn't intend to reunite with my mom. One person who knew him as well as anyone said, "They were never going to get back together."

Lark was mainly about the money, and my father was a fertile resource. Had she gotten wind of his desire to get married again but not to her, that he was entertaining the thought of reuniting with Sara, his second wife? Had she learned that the gravy train return to the good life had gotten derailed?

Even if that were all true, there remained the imponderable. Was revenge enough of a possible motive to make Mom a suspect? Was she even capable of such a monstrous thing?

The plot thickened when the Conway PD received an anonymous letter from someone who claimed investigation-neutrality and no involvement in the homicides. The letter included this statement: "YOU NEED TO LOOK AT ONE OF HIS EX-WIVES VERY CAREFULLY," closing with:

"The very innocent by nature is the demon in disguise."

The investigation was an impressive display of fact-finding. When it came to possible motives, investigators had produced a smorgasbord of selections. Which held the truth?

Investigators, I'd come to learn, strove to see the world through the eyes of witnesses to relive events prior to the crime. The problem here was too many eyes to see through, peering all over the place, sending investigators down many divergent paths. It was a maddening maze with no evident way out. Four weeks in, for all their considerable diligence and know-how, investigators hadn't found a clear way forward within a narrow scope of inquiry.

They say the truth will out. But would it here? Or would each path conclude in a dead end, banishing the case to a box-cramped, dust-filled cold basement in Conway, Arkansas? Through no fault of their own, investigators were, I think fair to say, stymied.

Then, seemingly out of nowhere, while probing eyes kept looking here and there, a tsunami came crashing in, tossing the investigation—and some personal worlds—on its head.

10

I BEGAN HAVING A RECURRING dream. The details never changed.

My father and I are driving alone in his Lexus on U.S. highway 64 which runs east-west along the northern boundary of Conway. He stares straight ahead, two hands on the wheel, a Rolex strapped on his left wrist and his glasses perched on his nose in that crooked way he always wore them, giving him that darling, studious look. He wears a white button-down collared shirt, the style of shirt he wore like a uniform, one button unfastened at the top, and meticulously starched collars lying flat at obedient attention.

As the car roars down the road, he keeps repeating he has to leave, and I plead with him to please stay. I keep begging, "please, please don't go, Daddy, it's not time for you to go, it's way too soon." We repeat the exchange over and over again, a two-person mantra—"I can't stay," "please don't leave"—until the car screeches to a halt and the dream abruptly ends.

Each time after the dream, I awake holding back tears, visualizing his face, blue eyes, and premature wrinkles. I pray he'll magically appear in my conscious world, materializing in my presence, so I can tell him he has an obligation to stay on this earth to be with me, to complete his job as my father. I want to tell him that the parent-child relationship is the most important unfinished business decent humans can have. I want to ask questions, get advice, soak up his wisdom, and receive his approval. I want to hug him. I want to feel the security of his embrace that only my father can provide. I want him to return and take care of things the way only he could. I want him to make things right again. I want him back.

I wondered whether the sense of loss I felt would burden me forever. Would it become a calcified cloud that persistently blocks light from reaching me? Or would I awake one morning and it'd be gone, like a nagging headache that times out? Maybe if the criminal investigation began to show promise, taking us down the road to justice, my spirits might get buoyed. As things stood, however, that seemed a long shot.

The psychology I kept hearing was that healing functioned with passing time, and that God would never put on me anything I couldn't handle. I found no comfort in that. The notion that the God I believed in thought I was strong enough to handle my father's murder was nothing short of overwhelming.

On June 18, 2002, I traveled to Arkansas to handle a variety of unfamiliar tasks and details regarding my father's estate. My brother Trey wanted to handle them alone, but I insisted on equal involvement and worry. I had been going through the mere motions of living the past four weeks, floating around in a daze, half-conscious, half-numb, trying to get a handle on a world without my father. Taking care of estate matters gave my life purpose and made me feel functional. It also kept me connected to my father.

The last night of the visit, Thursday, June 20, my fiancé Cory and I spent time with my dear friend Ann in Little Rock. We went out on the town and had a good time, the first time since the funeral that I'd spent time unwinding and socializing. The injection of normal felt good.

The next day, Friday, June 21, mid-afternoon, I gave Ann a long hug goodbye, in her doorway, and Cory and I began to walk to the car to make our way to my brother's place in Conway. The door clicked closed behind her as Ann disappeared into her home.

Seconds later, before we could put our luggage in the car trunk, I heard the rumbling sounds of Ann running down the interior staircase leading to her front door. I turned as she flung open the door, and hollered that Trey was on the phone and needed to talk to me immediately. I couldn't imagine what was up. Trey and I had finished the important things we needed to do. We had nothing to discuss, certainly nothing that was time sensitive. Besides, we'd be at his place in thirty minutes. What possibly couldn't wait?

Ann handed me the phone with an anxious look.

"Yeah?"

"Ashley, Mom's missing."

"What do you mean 'missing'?"

"She didn't show up for work today." He paused, apparently waiting for me to respond to that shocking nugget of information. I couldn't get words out. "And"—he continued—"she isn't answering her phone."

"Who was the last person who talked to her?" I said.

"We don't know, maybe at work yesterday. No one knows where she is."

I told him I would make some phone calls before driving to Conway. He said he would do the same. Numerous phone calls later to family and friends, we hadn't found her or moved closer to where she might be. No one had heard from her. She had vanished, without a word.

It was beyond unusual. It was un-Lark like.

My mom never missed work. She never fell out of touch. She was a creature of rigid routine. She had been a dental hygienist for six years and loved her work. Without fail, she showed up each day with enthusiasm, no matter what was going on her life, no matter how shitty she felt. Most nights after work she'd go home, have a glass of wine and dinner, maybe do some laundry, before settling into the night with a book or a TV show. At this stage of her life, you could set a Timex by her movements.

Something had to be seriously wrong. Bad thoughts crept into my head. Please God, not again. Trey continued making calls while Cory and I resumed our trip to his house. As we left I turned to Ann and whispered, "I know it's Dick. I *know* it's him. He's done all this. It's him."

Ann spared me her own immediate thought, that my mother was probably dead.

When I got to Trey's, he and I called the Salt Lake City police and asked them to dispatch a unit to her condo. We stressed the urgency, that we feared our mother was in grave danger. We showed restraint and patience as they put us through the paces of their protocol questions, and after we answered each one as best we could, they backtracked on us. She hadn't been missing long enough to warrant their involvement. Their policy required twenty-four hours before they'd invest their precious resources in our little problem.

I wasn't having it.

"Please, please, go to her condo. You don't understand. She's in danger. Her life might depend on your getting there now. She isn't someone who disappears. Something is wrong."

A strange power filled me. I wasn't freaking out. I didn't get wild. I didn't cry. I was focused and determined like never before. I had a single, exclusive life mission at that moment: saving my mother. I wasn't getting off the phone until they agreed to go to the condo. I wasn't letting up. I met every "but" from them with a "you must."

After much gnashing of teeth, they relented and promised to send a couple of officers to the condo. We gave them the address and the combination code to the front door, and authorized their entry.

Less than thirty minutes later, they called. They couldn't gain entry. The code didn't work. I suspected human error. They knocked on the door several times and got no answer. We told them to break in, smash the door down if necessary. This wasn't the time to stand on ceremony. She could be shot, dying inside. They sent someone else out and managed to get inside. As I said, human error.

My mother wasn't there. The apartment was clean and showed no signs of a struggle. Nor was there a suicide note.

I had given the police a list of irregularities to look for—an unmade bed, dishes in the sink, and untidy rooms. Chaos and mess didn't exist within the orbit of my Mom's personal universe. She was OCD when it came to an orderly home. She made clean and tidy an art form. That is why she got turned inside out when she saw how Conte lived, prompting her to pull the rug out from under his fantasy love story and ending their marriage. Household chaos made her skin crawl.

Sure enough, a dish and glass were in the sink. More telling, the bed was unmade, which in all my time on this earth I can't recall ever happening with her. Ever. She made the bed every day before going to work as if she were in military boot camp. To her, a made-up bed first thing in the morning was essential—like oxygen.

The bottom sheet was still on the bed, but the comforter was folded back toward the front and, more revealing, the top sheet and pillowcases were removed. Policed found the latter items soaked and sitting inside the dryer. Someone had run them through a wash cycle, removed them, and placed them in the dryer, but for some reason, hadn't pushed a button to finish the chore. I couldn't imagine it was my Mom.

They didn't find a purse. Travel necessities like toothbrush, toothpaste, and other toiletries were missing from their normal places in the bathroom. They couldn't locate her passport. The bedroom dresser drawers were empty and a pile of clothing was stacked to the side. It looked like someone hastily grabbed a bunch of clothes while bolting out the door.

An email message was found, unsent, on her computer:

"I'm running to spend my life planning cocktail parties onboard a mega yacht that cruises the Caribbean and Mediterranean. I cannot let this opportunity pass me by. It is the life I was meant to live, that of a queen. It was the acting job of my life to hide this from all of you until I was gone. That's why I moved from Carson City at the end of February, because I didn't think I could hide it from Dr. Dick. The prerequisite is that I walk away clean from my family, friends, job, and life in Salt Lake. If I end up old and penniless, I'll be looking you all up again. Lark."

The inspection intensified. Police found a printout of an internet search for flights to Florida and the Caribbean. They also found my mother's car parked in its designated spot, which usually would be unremarkable, but in this increasingly bizarre situation, the location of the car was consistent with her fleeing, or something worse. The police called airlines and travel agencies to find a record of a flight booked in her name. They came up empty.

They tried to interview neighbors, knocking on the doors to the other five units in the building. They found some at home, but none had seen or heard anything.

The police had been unable to contact any person with knowledge of my mother's whereabouts. She had flown the coop without detection.

By this point, the Salt Lake City police felt they'd done what they could. I was betting they concluded my mom was a live one—not far off, I know—and she was gallivanting about on a wild party spree.

I had one more thought. I asked them if they'd finally survey the jogging trail at Sugarhouse Park, a short distance away, where my mother often ran during the early evening after work, sometimes stopping at Bally's to use weights and machines, before completing the run back home. I had never felt particularly safe running that trail, and avoided it at night, and didn't like her using it at night. They gave lip service to my plea and said were headed back to the station and to alert them if anything new cropped up. I took that as a no answer. We were now on our own.

I remembered what Dick Conte whispered to me the day of the ill-advised wedding, that he'd always be there for us if anything happened to Mom. Time to find Dick and cash in on the promise. I first called the hospital where he worked. They wouldn't disclose his whereabouts. It wasn't public information. But I insisted. I was his "stepdaughter." It wasn't technically true—the divorce had become final the month before—but I figured I had license to split hairs in the circumstances. It worked. They told me he had "called in sick."

Fuck! Those three words hit like me a swift kick to the gut. I felt like throwing up. My mind reeled. I could only think of one thing. I didn't say it. I couldn't stand to hear the words. Trey didn't say it. But we both thought it.

I tried other numbers I had for Conte, and eventually he answered the phone with a meek, "Hello." I exploded with panic.

"Where is my mother!? Where is my mother!? She's missing! Where is she?!"

He paused. I could hear him take a deep breath. The exhale caused me to tilt my ear slightly away from the phone.

"She met a man in a bar in Park City last night." His voice was calm, his pace deliberate like he was pulling words off a teleprompter. "She took him home, slept with him, and then murdered him. I took her to the Mexican border and gave her some money so she could disappear. She's in big trouble."

"You're a fucking liar!" I didn't wait for a response. "Where is my mother?!" I screamed.

"Ashley, please calm down." His voice began to quiver. "Don't call the police. I don't know where she is. She is hiding out somewhere."

"Too late! I've already called them. Where is my mother?! Where is my mother?!" I was screaming so loud I set off the security alarm in Trey's house.

Conte started back up with the same answer, "I don't know where she . . ." but I hung up.

Shortly after the call, this email landed in my inbox: "Ashley, I'm in hiding. Did a terrible thing. . . . Can't talk about it on e-mail. Tell everyone that I ran away with a rich man in his mega-yacht and had to walk away from family, friends, and job. . . . Love you and Trey but I can't go to prison. Love Mother on the run."

I had last spoken to my mother two days before, on Wednesday evening, June 19. She was as she always was, home relaxing after work and a workout session at the gym. Our conversation was garden variety catch-up, nothing that would qualify as front page family news. Since my father's death we had talked more often and gotten closer. During the call she didn't betray a hint of stress or concern or any hidden agenda. If anything momentous was percolating, I was sure I'd have detected some rattling between the lines.

Investigative files illuminate the hours prior to my mother's disappearance: she had an uneventful workday at Pinebrook Dental on Thursday, June 20, arriving at 8:30 a.m. per normal. She handled her routine hygienist tasks, ate half her packed lunch, left work slightly after 5:00 p.m., jumped in her car, and arrived home about 5:30. She parked in her designated spot, grabbed her things—her lunch box, purse, and other items—and climbed three flights on the open stairwell to the top floor and her condo.

Upon entering her two-bedroom unit, she called out to her cat as she unloaded what she was carrying onto the kitchen counter. After placing everything down, out of the corner of her eye she saw a shadow emerging from her bedroom. She instinctively pivoted in that direction to face someone heading rapidly toward her. It was a man, hefty and tall, a black ski mask covering his face, dark rubber gloves on both hands, a floppy green military combat hat on his head, clothed in green pants and shirt and dark military boots. He had a gun in his right hand with a clip, scope and silencer, and a stun gun in his left, about two feet long, both black. She made a slight instinctive move toward the front door, but he was on her quickly, backing her into the kitchen corner and pinning her against the counter.

She began screaming. Raising the gun, the perpetrator told her to "stop screaming." When she didn't, he placed the gun on the counter and put his hand over her mouth to muffle her voice. He told her again, "be quiet . . . or I'll kill you." She complied and he retrieved the gun. She stole a glance at the clock. It read 5:45 p.m.

Using his gun as a pointer, the perpetrator had her move toward the bedroom, holding the back of her arm as he pressed her along. Once inside the bedroom, he told her to sit in a yellow wingback chair that had been moved from its customary spot against a side wall to the middle of the bedroom, like a performance prop. A pile of thick red rope, the kind used to tie boats docked at harbors, lay on the seat of the chair like a coiled snake.

She refused to sit. She told him, "You might as well shoot me, I'm not getting in that chair all tied up." He pointed the gun at her. She took a seat. She started to scream again, expressing fear he intended to tie the rope around her neck. He promised he wouldn't. She stopped screaming. She pleaded that he not tie her up too tight. He agreed to loosen the grip of the ropes if she wouldn't scream any more. He wrapped the red rope around her chest and the back of the chair, leaving her hands to dangle free.

Then he presented her with a small Tupperware jar filled with clear red liquid, about half a cup in volume. He ordered she drink it. She asked about the contents. He replied, "cough syrup, Ativan and vodka." She refused to drink. She told him she wasn't going to poison herself. His response was silent and swift: he put the gun to her head.

She continued to resist. She said if she was about to die, she'd rather he shoot her and get it over with it. She wasn't drinking poison. He assured her it wasn't poison. It would only sedate her. To prove the point, he took a small swig. She still refused. This time he said, "If you don't, I am going to kill you right now." She downed the concoction.

Fifteen minutes later she began to get groggy and shortly, passed out. She awoke hours later in the back of a truck making its way down a highway. Her bra and panties had been removed. Her blouse was on backwards. She was trapped with two sets of handcuffs, one restricting her hands in front of her body and the other binding her legs to a clasp in the truck cabin. The sets of cuffs were looped together. Suitcases were strewn around her, including two of her own. She managed to open her suitcases to find several of her items, including cosmetics, a bathing suit, shoes, jewelry, scarves, CDs, medicine, her hygienist license, her passport, bank records, payroll checks, and books.

She felt around the bed of the truck and located a tire iron. Her hands still cuffed, she lifted the tire iron and, through the rear opening between the front and back truck cabins, tried to strike her kidnapper. She couldn't reach him, managing only to graze the driver-side headrest. Her kidnapper yanked the tire iron from her and shot her several times in the arm with the stun gun, putting an end to her attempts to disable him. She passed out again.

Several hours later she awoke in a cabin in the woods, hands cuffed and wrapped around a bedpost. Nighttime was approaching. She looked around to locate her kidnapper. He wasn't there. She called out. He entered the room and made her take another Ativan. He picked up his gun and held it across his chest. She knew she didn't have long to live.

11

FEELING POWERLESS IN THE FACE of the most horrific thing imaginable about to happen is terrifying. I kept trying to drive gruesome scenarios from my mind. They kept insisting on coming back in. It was an internal battle like none I'd experienced.

In the balance lay any sense of hope. But while an ally, hope can be a fragile flower and it was withering away with every breath. If hope took flight, panic was sure to swoop in and take its place, and we'd become immobilized. It was a gut-wrenching feeling. I eagerly awaited the next revelation.

After getting virtually nowhere with the Salt Lake City police, except finding possible clues they never would have unearthed on their own, for Trey and me, time had become an even more critical factor. Something had to break soon. Otherwise, my mother likely would be dead, assuming she wasn't already.

If we'd had any doubt before, it was gone. Neither the unsent email the police found in the condo nor the email I received came from my mom. There is nothing about either of the letters that spoke Lark Elliott. It wasn't her style of writing and the message was so beyond the pale, even for her, that we were sure someone else had written them. We were confident, at least I was, that the someone else was

Dick Conte. I knew in my heart that Conte had taken our Mom and was contemplating evil.

We had to contact Dick again because, until we learned otherwise, our road to Mom was through him. I grabbed Trey's landline phone to call. Trey raised his hand. After the first call I made to Conte, when my voice became a screech, Trey was concerned about me going at Conte again. He proposed to play good cop to my bad cop. I was cool with that.

He placed his call and Conte answered again. Trey spoke gently but firmly and told Conte how worried we were, how he'd said he would always be there for us, and we needed his help—and blah, blah, blah. Good job, Trey. Conte fessed up. My mother wasn't in Mexico. She was there. He admitted he had handcuffed and drugged her.

Perhaps now realizing what he'd admitted, he took a different tack. He threatened to kill her. He threatened to kill himself. It would be a classic murder-suicide.

Trey began to plead with him. "Please don't hurt my mother. My father was murdered thirty days ago."

Conte weakened. Now he promised he wouldn't harm her. He began to cry and scream that he was "gonna kill myself" and that "his life was worthless." Silently, I wanted Trey to encourage that plan of action. Let the piece of shit blow his pathetic brains out. But Trey kept talking to him, pleading not to harm our mother, staying on message. Each time Conte threatened the kill himself, I wanted Trey to say, "Yeah, sounds like the right thing to do." But Trey kept saying, "No, don't do that. Just be calm. Don't kill yourself. We just want you to let our mother go. We want her to be safe."

After a bit, Trey convinced Conte to put my mother on the phone. She was groggy but composed and seemed otherwise fine. She told Trey that Conte had tried to give her hot dogs and beer but she declined. I couldn't imagine what she had gone through.

Trey handed the phone to me.

"Mom, are you okay?"

"Yes, sweetie. I'm fine. I'm just here." She slurred, sounding stoned or drunk in the extreme.

"What are you doing?" I tried to sound normal, but it wasn't easy. My heart was beating like a conga drum.

"Dick's trying to get me to eat a hot dog and drink a Corona, but I'm not hungry."

"Mom, I love you."

"Love you too, sweetie."

"Here's Trey." I handed the phone to my brother.

"Hey Mom, you still okay?" Trey said.

She answered she was.

"Put Dick back on the phone." We wanted Conte engaged with us, the children. Maybe there was a sweet spot somewhere buried inside him.

While they spoke, I retrieved my mobile phone and placed a call of my own, to 911 in Nevada. We had confirmation of the kidnapping. There could be no justification now for law enforcement to sit back. It was time for them to take control.

The dispatcher picked up on the first ring.

"What is your emergency?" The female voice asked.

"My mother's been kidnapped."

"Your mother's been what? I can hardly hear you, you're talking very, very low." She seemed annoyed.

"She's been kidnapped! She's going to die if you don't find her; she's at Dr. Dick Conte's house, and he lives in Carson City, Nevada." I was losing patience. This was my first 911 experience. I felt super eager but isolated.

"She's handcuffed and drugged and she's on the phone with my brother right now. If you don't find her, he will kill her."

"Okay, you think she's at his house, right?"

"I *know* she's at his house! I'm telling you he's going to kill her and he's going to kill himself."

"Do you have an address?"

"An address? Carson City? Can't you look it up? Dr. Dick Conte. He's an ER doctor. Carson Tahoe Hospital. People know him."

"We need specific information to pass on to local police. Hold on for a second."

I could hear them making fun of me in the background, as if this were some big joke, like I was an escaped mental health patient with a stolen phone. They didn't seem to believe me. It was hurtful, and I was furious. I was doing my best to stay focused and not explode.

"You still there?" She said when back on the line.

Jesus! "Yes, I'm still here. Look, Conte has multiple guns, machetes, cameras, grenades, knives, hidden crawl spaces, and all sorts of military weapons. He's a trained killer! Please send someone out there now. It is a matter of life and death."

"It'd help if we had an address." The tone had more than a ring of sarcasm.

"It's not a home. It's a cabin. It's in the woods. Hold on. Hold on. Wait a minute. . . Jeffery Pine Road, near Old Clear Creek and Highway 50. That's it. Send someone there now . . . please." I managed to hold back tears, but they were gushing forth.

That is where it ended. It was wing-and-prayer time. Trey and I feared that if the 911 call didn't incite law enforcement into action, my mother's life would likely depend on our ability to talk the nutcase Conte down from his tree, long distance. After I got off the phone with the charming woman at 911, however, Conte told Trey he had to make another call and hung up.

At about 7:15 p.m., Conte evidently called Ann Cobb, a nurse with whom he worked at the hospital. He was crying when she picked the phone. He told Cobb my mother had filed for divorce. He asked Cobb if she'd be willing to come over to get his dogs and take care of them, since he wouldn't be able to do so for a while. She agreed, and immediately contacted Cecilia Dodson, a friend and another nurse, to go with her. Cobb had a bad feeling.

About this time, I got a call from Solon Blake of the Douglas County Sheriff's Office (DCSO). The 911 lady had come through after all. Officer Blake put a bunch of questions to me and I eagerly gave him answers, each time stressing the urgency of the moment. I supplemented my answers, telling him Conte owned two vehicles, a large silver Dodge pickup with a camper shell and an older red Jeep with a snowplow on the front. I warned him about the massive Conte weapons collection, which he seemed aware of somehow. We ended the call.

A few minutes later, Blake called me back with follow-up questions. Trey was back on the phone with Conte. When I shared that with Blake, he told me to tell Trey silently to keep Conte on the line as long as possible, using small talk or whatever he could to keep him engaged on a low-key level. They would get there soon. It was approaching 7:30.

While I was speaking with Blake, Trey told me that Conte put him on hold to take another call, which I relayed to Blake. The call apparently came from our uncle Kevin Clark, the longstanding Conte bosom buddy. More cooks were entering the kitchen. Uncle Kevin now tried to calm Conte down and talk him out of whatever he was planning to do. But the situation hadn't otherwise changed.

Officer Blake then called Uncle Kevin, who said Conte appeared to be having a "psychotic episode" and his behavior "was very uncharacteristic." He emphasized to Blake that Conte had "extensive weapons and military experience and could potentially be very dangerous." He also told Blake that Conte admitted that when he'd initially accosted my mother, he was wearing a black ski mask and armed with an electronic stun gun. He also admitted that he gave my mother the choice of drinking the Ativan-laced concoction or suffer the power of the stun gun.

At 7:50, Conte informed Trey he no longer intended to harm either my mother or himself. He also told Trey he had freed my mother from the handcuffs. This appeared to be a major breakthrough, but we took little comfort. We knew our mother could be overpowered by this maniacally unstable person with a military arsenal. None of his assurances had the thinnest reed of reliability. He was dangerous.

Trey called Officer Blake to let him know about the new turn of events. He implored Blake to try to contact our mother and Conte. Blake advised they were reluctant to take any action that might endanger our Mom or their deputies until all "necessary resources were in place." They were worried about Conte's firepower which, in a hostage situation, multiplied the risks.

Meanwhile, Ann Cobb and Cecilia Dodson arrived at the cabin. Conte was outside on the phone with his mother. When the two women drew near to him, he handed the phone to Cobb and asked her to talk with his mother. Cobb was confused and taken aback, but she obliged. Dick Conte's mother, a highly-regarded community volunteer in Wisconsin—the apple there bounced down the hill way far from that tree—expressed concern for both her son and my mother. That confused Cobb. Why did Conte's mother mention my mom, whom she assumed was in Salt Lake City? After getting off the phone, Ann inquired about my mom, and Conte said she was in the cabin. The nurse went inside to find her, but she wasn't there. Ann didn't notice the two syringes full of lethal liquid in the bathroom that Conte had set aside, for himself and my mom.

Law enforcement moved into action. They had devised a plan based on the working assumption that Conte owned "an extensive weapons collection and had combat and tactical experience," was "an accomplished sniper," and allegedly, "a contract mercenary" who had conducted "secret operations for various governments," including in Afghanistan and Grenada. They were informed Conte might have "more than two hundred guns."

They dispatched a patrol unit to the intersection of Old Clear Creek and Highway 395, which Conte could reach with relative ease if he tried to flee and gain access to Highway 50. If he could reach Highway 50, he'd enjoy the maximum speed limit and a long stretch of driving road. The patrol unit was to stay out of sight of the cabin but close enough to assure no cars left undetected. The deputies found a curvature in the road that provided concealment and a good sight line. They stood by.

DCSO dispatched a second patrol car from the Carson City Sheriff's Office to Highway 50 near a gated community to the north of the cabin. The deputy in that car contacted local residents to obtain the gate code so he could secure a concealed place to watch comings and goings, should Conte try to access Highway 50 and go northwest instead.

DCSO placed a third patrol unit at the Carson Tahoe Hospital in the event Conte escaped undetected and showed up there. While that seemed an unlikely event, the hospital was his workplace, so it was a safe place for him, and it was at least feasible he might try to retreat there.

The DCSO also activated its Crisis Negotiation Team (CNT), which included a psychologist to provide mental health observations and suggest appropriate dialogue for law enforcement team members.

Because of the extreme danger Conte posed with his weaponry arsenal, the DCSO assembled its Special Operations Response Team (SORT), a 24-7 group to respond to extreme situations and handle the transport of high-risk prisoners on an on-call basis.

Both CNT and SORT were told to be ready at the designated command center at DCSO headquarters, pending developments. For the time being, the DCSO wanted to stay in touch with Trey and me to get updates from our phone contact with Conte and our mom. Deploying CNT or SORT was premature, but their opportunity could come in a flash.

Finally, the DCSO assigned three patrol vehicles to go directly to the cabin. They were on their way and would be there soon.

When she didn't see my mom in the cabin, Ann Cobb started to search the property. She went out back and scanned. The sun was setting and visibility waning. She didn't see Mom. Nor did she see the two empty and waiting open graves Conte had dug for himself and my mother.

She noticed that the truck's driver's side door was open. She walked over and took a peek inside. My mom wasn't there. She then noticed one of the back doors slightly ajar. She went to take a look inside where she found my mother, lying unmoving atop duffel bags. Ann called to her. My mother raised her head and said hello. The nurse asked her what had happened. My mother explained generally the course of wretched events during the past twenty-four hours. Mom then got up and started organizing her possessions that Conte had stuffed into suitcases at the condo. Ann said she'd take Mom wherever she wanted. My mom said she'd like to go to a hotel.

While they were talking, Conte came out back. He grabbed a few bags from the back of the truck and moved them, ignoring the two women. Conte made another trip to move bags and my mother and Ann saw him crying. Mom told Ann that if left alone, he'd likely kill himself. Conte looked over and said, "How can anyone be married for only ninety days?" Ann responded, "Look, Dick, Lark is coming with me," and Conte replied, "That's probably best." Ann helped my mother move her things into the Jeep.

Cecilia was on the front steps of the cabin watching over the dogs. When my mother emerged from the back with Ann, she saw Mom crying. She stood up and gave my mom a long hug. Ann told her the game plan and Cecilia said she'd stay with Conte in case he started talking again about killing himself. Conte joined the three women in the front of the cabin. As my mother got ready to leave, she and Conte hugged, each saying, "I'm sorry."

Ann and my mother got in the car and drove toward a hotel. After thirty seconds of silence, my mother turned to Ann and said, "I hope Cecilia doesn't get hurt." Ann didn't reply. A few seconds later, my mother again expressed concern that Conte might do something violent. She wanted to return to the cabin and make sure nothing bad happened. Ann didn't know what to do. She started to shake and felt shock coming on. She thought she'd better call her husband. While trying to scroll through the phone to get her husband's phone number and simultaneously drive, she reconsidered making the call. She thought they should call Cecilia to say the situation was too dangerous to be there alone with Dick, and they would return to get her. They were about a mile from the cabin.

Meanwhile, the three patrol vehicles were dispatched to the cabin and passed the Jeep driving eastbound as Mom and Ann continued to equivocate about what to do. The police noticed the Jeep, called in the situation, and coordinated an action plan. One patrol vehicle continued to the cabin and the other two turned around to follow the Jeep.

As Ann fumbled with the phone, a glare hit her eyes as police lights from behind bounced off the driver's sideview mirror. Already stressed out, she started to lose control of the Jeep due to the sudden glare. She frantically tried to regain control. Slowing the car down, she tried to turn the engine off, but she was unfamiliar with the Jeep and inadvertently let the clutch out, causing the vehicle to roll forward haphazardly.

The next thing the two women heard was an amplified voice commanding them to put their "hands outside the window." Ann hit the brakes and they complied with the command. Police then directed that "the driver step out of the vehicle." Ann tried, but when she did, the Jeep started to roll again. The police screamed, "Put the vehicle in gear!" She was stunned and afraid and disabled from responding. My mom reached over and helped her put the Jeep in gear. Ann stepped out of the Jeep with her hands raised. It was 8:01 p.m.

The officers directed Ann to walk backwards toward the flashing lights of the patrol car. When she got close, the officers handcuffed her arms behind her, explaining she wasn't under arrest. The officer clamped the cuffs so tight it brought severe pain. They put Ann in the back seat of the patrol car.

Next they commanded my mother to get out of the Jeep. They followed the same routine for her, putting her in handcuffs and placing her with Ann in the back seat of the patrol car. When my mom settled in, Ann noticed that my mother's wrists were red and swollen.

The officers began to ask Mom questions. She was slow to respond, and when she did, provided a mishmash of incoherent phrases. The DCSO summoned paramedics to the scene.

Several minutes later, at 8:07, Deputy Gonzalez of the DCSO, driving to the house in the patrol car that passed the Jeep on the highway, pulled close to the cabin. As he pulled into the driveway, he noticed a male step off the porch and wave him down, as if flagging for help. He stopped the car, got out, and identified the man as Richard Conte, whom he detained without incident.

Gonzalez interrogated Conte about what was in the cabin, specifically asking about trip wires, booby traps, and explosives. Law enforcement was tentative about entering the cabin, knowing what they did about the Conte armory. Conte denied any trip wires and booby traps.

Minutes later, an FBI Special Agent, and personnel with the Tahoe Douglas Bomb Squad arrived, as did the entire SORT group that DCSO assigned earlier.

After a debriefing, they had Gonzalez—who appeared to have rapport with Conte—ask the man in custody for permission to search the cabin. Conte balked, however, saying he was reluctant to grant consent to search the house for anything except people. Agreeing to the limitation, SORT personnel went inside and found Cecilia unharmed, albeit half-petrified.

SORT took command of the situation. They cuffed Conte, put him in a patrol car, and transported him to the DCSO jail. At 2:50 a.m., June 22, the DCSO booked Conte on charges of kidnapping.

As Conte was en route to the local jail, paramedics from the East Fork Fire Department (EFFD) arrived to evaluate my mother. After checking her out, EFFD personnel transported her to Carson Valley Medical Center in Gardnerville.

Trey and I got word from DCSO that Mom was safe and en route to get medically checked out. My poor mother. I couldn't begin to relate to what she had gone through. I worried about the long-term impact.

She was tough, no question, and when I spoke with her while she was at the cabin, she seemed remarkably grounded and at ease, despite the ordeal and drug impact. But you never know about trauma. It can be sinister. It has no compassion.

My personal relief was beyond description. But I also felt thoroughly beaten down emotionally. The combination was exhausting.

I wondered if the family was cursed. I began to fear that this latest incident was but a horrible round two of a prolonged miserable existence. Were we destined to a life of continuous pain and suffering?

The silver lining I perceived was the positive effect Conte's failed kidnapping gambit would have on the stalled criminal investigation into the murders of my father and Timmy Wayne. I thought its revelation was clear as a cloudless day. Despite all the horror he visited upon my mother, Conte had committed a major misstep and given us a gift. His perverse madness, or as my uncle Kevin so affectionately put it, "psychotic episode," had been exposed, which, I assumed, would throw the doors to justice wide open.

More naïve I could not have been.

12

BY OUTWARD APPEARANCES, MY MOTHER seemed largely unscathed by the kidnapping nightmare, although I detected hints of hardness in her eyes. I assumed emotional scars from something like that would take time to quietly form below the surface. She had the inner strength to cope and I expected her to move forward with her characteristic courage. Still, I worried she might become more tentative and less playful and, even worse, more mistrustful. I worried as well where the experience might leave us as mother and daughter.

I knew she harbored fear and anxiety that Conte might again try to get at her, that he had unfinished business. But he was behind bars, and from what we were told, he wasn't going anywhere soon. We were all safe now, weren't we?

Me, I felt untethered from the world. My mind had a new tendency to wander, drifting from its moorings, floating from activity to activity as if under the grip of a spell. In conversations, I'd space out zombie-like, and when people noticed, they'd say, "You okay?" I always came back with, "Yeah, I'm fine." But I wasn't fine. I was melancholy and confused, unable to understand why all this was happening, what it meant, and what might happen yet still. Emotionally, I swung back and forth, like on a vine, between anxious and sad, sad and angry, and angry and depressed. I wanted to cry a lot. I wanted to lash out.

I had a wedding coming up, but that now had a secondary feel, no longer an eagerly anticipated high point of a life. It almost seemed burdensome, like something I had on my to-do list to check off. I worried about my ability to get up for the cherished event and revel in the fullness of the happiness and joy it potentially held, especially without my father to walk me down the aisle and with my mother, through no fault of her own, possibly unable to rise to the occasion.

I struggled to see a horizon bringing a brighter day. I saw plenty of darkness and webs of complexity, and I was eager to know what the legal system had in store, both in the kidnapping and murder matters. I began to realize that the halls of justice might hold the key to my emotional wellbeing and could liberate me from the terror of the past several weeks. I certainly didn't know what to expect from the legal system. It intimidated me, and until the process played out, I assumed I'd wallow in a prolonged limbo, at the mercy of a system over which I had no control, an archaic world with its own language, rules, biases, and priorities.

Questions began to hit me. Was justice a real thing or the stuff of movies? What if justice wasn't enough? What if it failed me entirely? Did it matter because I had no choice but to succumb to its power and pray for the best? Did I have the emotional fortitude and stamina to ride it out? What happens if I don't? What will my family look like after the legal machinery spit us out at the other end?

A small part of me envisioned more roses than thorns. I assumed that Conte's goose was cooked in Nevada because of the kidnapping. So the open question was the murder investigation, where he now had to be the prime—if not sole—suspect. I had a vision. I imagined the lead Conway investigator, eraser in one hand, strolling to the white board that listed the theories and possible suspects they'd harvested, ceremoniously wiping the board clean, and with a felt marker in the other hand, writing with long bold strokes, "Richard Ralph Conte. M.D."

I mean, what more did anyone need to know? To me, it was plain as day. Conte killed my father and Timmy Wayne. How did anyone at this point doubt that?

That is not to say I thought Conte would lie down. I got how the system worked. The accused digs in and defends hard, throwing up smoke and creating the uncertainty needed to leverage a deal or improve chances of an acquittal after a battle before a jury of his peers. "Truth" in the criminal justice system, I would learn, is a moving target, and dangerously so when in the hands of a clever magician who boasts a law license.

The good doctor didn't help his cause. His kidnapping escapade breathed life into a homicide investigation on life support. It was as if he'd called out, "Come get me; I'm your man." He was also dumb enough to allow Nevada investigators to interview him without counsel present on the night he was captured, a privilege he also granted to Arkansas investigators a few days later, although he brought counsel that time as a prop. My guess is, Conte sweet-talked his attorney into thinking the whole thing was a misunderstanding and not to worry. Take a seat, counselor, and let me handle the seasoned investigators. The banty rooster has it under control.

Conte denied ever visiting Arkansas—ever—and flat-out denied any involvement in the murders, adding he "never met" my father. He added that, at the time of the murders, he thought my father lived in San Francisco with his second wife. He wouldn't have even heard about the homicides, he represented, but for his best friend Kevin Clark, my uncle, who called him with the tragic news the night of May 19, after I had told Clark.

But he also made several denials regarding what happened in Salt Lake City and Nevada with my mother that spoke volumes about his relationship with the truth.

He denied my mother was frightened when he cornered her in the condo, claiming that after she saw him initially, "she calmed down almost immediately." He disclaimed any of the hysterical screaming my mother described. He denied wearing a mask, tying her in the chair with the red rope, forcing her to drink the drug-infused cocktail (which he "offered" her, presumably like a gentleman offers a cocktail to a lady at a bar), and coercing her into the truck to go to Nevada, stating she "voluntarily" joined him for the trip "in no uncertain terms."

My mother's imagination, if he was to be believed, was wildly fertile.

He also claimed she willingly agreed to occupy the bed of the truck for the several-hour, six-hundred-mile grueling trip, not because he forced and restrained her there—he initially denied handcuffing her—but because he preferred to have his "dogs up front." How gallant. Besides, he explained, my mother was "very sleepy" and the cozy confines of the truck bed gave her "a place to lie down."

My mother, who fancied herself a bit of a queen and was single-minded about enjoying the better things in life, was evidently content to languish for several hours in the middle of the night on the metal floor in the bed of a truck roaring down a highway. I guess I didn't know my mom as well as I thought.

Later he reversed himself, admitting he handcuffed Mom to the bed of the truck, explaining he took that extraordinary step not to advance a wicked scheme, but to keep my mother from jumping out of the truck while it was moving. Ponder that. He purportedly stopped the truck, after divining she had changed her mind about joining him on the excursion, overcame her in the back, and restrained her for the first time, all to prevent her from performing the herculean task of jumping out of a truck bed that was barreling down an interstate highway.

By the time of the interviews, investigators had not discovered either the lethal syringes or the ready-and-waiting graves. That might explain why, when they asked Conte if he threatened to kill my mother and he emphatically said, "Absolutely not," they didn't fall off their chairs. Later he highlighted the denial: "I never, at any time, said . . . I would kill her." He also denied threatening to kill himself, recasting what others said by claiming all he said was, "My life, as I know it, is over."

I guess we chalk up my mother's contrary contentions to drama queen rantings, and the syringes and dug graves to ghoulish theatrical props for creative playacting between lovers.

Investigators in Nevada moved quickly to obtain a warrant to search Conte's cabin. As they did, the Conway PD, alerted to the kidnapping, declared their own interest in the effort. Until the kidnapping, Conte had not been on the radar of the homicide investigation. He wasn't even a dot on the screen. The kidnapping changed that in an instant, thrusting Conte onto center stage.

Working together, the two police departments recrafted a new and broader warrant to rope in potential evidence to aid both investigations. In addition, the Conway PD dispatched investigators to Nevada to assist in the search and coordinate investigative efforts. Unwittingly, Conte had managed to contribute to an investigative breakthrough.

The search started on June 25, 2002 and lasted two days. It included the cabin and Conte's diesel truck. We were told that the searches turned up a bounty of material, and investigators were pleased with the progress. How pleased they wouldn't say.

I knew that the homicide case had gaps that were unlikely to get filled. There were no witnesses. There were no fingerprints. There was no DNA. There were no recovered weapons. Investigators also wouldn't likely get a ballistics match. And, as time went on, additional unanswered questions would arise. And there would be the Conte alibi gambit, revealed later.

Meanwhile, the State of Nevada moved forward with their case against Conte. They charged him with committing three Class B felonies: Count One, kidnapping with the use of a deadly weapon; Count Two, unlawful administering of a controlled substance; and Count Three, possession of stolen property.

At the October 15, 2002 arraignment, Conte pled not guilty to each count. Two months later, however, Conte got religion and made a deal with prosecutors. In exchange for his guilty plea to modified charges, the State of Nevada agreed to strike the deadly weapon enhancement language from the kidnapping charge, and dismiss in its entirety the stolen property charge. The kidnapping charge, less the enhancement, remained, as did the original Count Two, for illegally administering a controlled substance.

Amended Count One carried a potential sentence of two to fifteen years in state prison and a maximum fine of $15,000. Count Two carried a potential sentence of one to six years and a maximum fine of $20,000. In the discretion of the Court, the sentences could run either concurrently or consecutively. If they ran consecutively, Conte could be sentenced to twenty-one years, with a maximum fine of $35,000. To our disappointment, the prosecution supported concurrent sentencing.

At the plea agreement hearing, the Court was tasked with assessing the deal. The judge began asking Conte why he was pleading guilty.

"To avoid going through a trial and confronting the people that I have to deal with," he responded. In other words, he was pleading guilty to a major felony not because he did anything wrong, but to be spared discomfort. The judge had thrown him a softball question and he botched it. He hadn't come to terms with his heinous crimes. To my novice mind, he was supposed to fall on his sword, admit he did something bad and unlawful and deserved judicially mandated consequences. Didn't his attorney walk him through the script?

The Court tried a different tack. The judge asked him what caused him to get charged with kidnapping. He responded that he became "distraught over opening a wedding present" and "wanted to get back together with my estranged wife."

He still wasn't getting it, and was struggling to stay on message. The record was getting muddled. If he continued to waver, the plea deal might be in jeopardy.

The Court wasn't about to let him off the hook. The judge interjected again, explaining to Conte that he hadn't said anything about a crime. In a polite way, the judge was letting him know he was evading the questions. The Court expected him to say what conduct he committed that formed the crime to which he was pleading guilty.

Conte responded that the drugs he administered to my mother "made her go along with me" and he "managed to convince her to come back with me and en route she changed her mind and I continued to drive, even though she changed her mind."

One step forward, two steps back. The latest answer was more consistent with innocence than guilt, or at a minimum a mixture of both. Now, he hadn't kidnapped her after all, at least not in the beginning. She had come with him voluntarily after he spiked her drink, as if they were partying, and then en route to a different party venue she changed her mind, after bouncing around in the back of a truck.

The hearing was at risk of going off the rails. Maybe this was a snapshot of the criminal mind, a contorted rearrangement of history. Maybe it's what happens to someone who has drunk their own Kool-Aid and, brimming with a self-crafted fantasy image, has told so many lies he has lost the ability to know the difference between non-fiction and fiction.

None of this was lost on the Court. The judge was steadfast and not about to let the hearing go sideways. Better he feed Conte the words.

"Did you kidnap this lady?"

"Yes, I think." He thinks? He's not sure? Time for judicial teeth pulling.

"That's the issue, isn't it?"

"Yes." Incredible. A tooth pulled.

"Shall we just use those words?" Isn't that how you talk to a three-year-old?

"Yes. I kidnapped my estranged wife." *Voila.*

"Did you inappropriately administer drugs to her? A simple 'yes' will suffice here."

"I gave her oral medication that she took, yes." The innocence thing again! He was regressing, causing the judge to drill down with him.

"Is she a patient of yours?" The judge was treating him like a witness who needed to be cajoled and boxed in. A "no" answer would move things along nicely.

"She has been at one time or another." He still wasn't getting it.

"Was she [a patient] the day you kidnapped her?" The corral door was closing.

"No." Baby steps to progress.

"Do you suppose that's inappropriate administration of a controlled substance?"

"Yes, it is." Excruciating, but done.

To assist with sentencing, the Court received a forensic psychological report that counsel for Conte had requested, and twenty-nine letters of support. The image of Conte that emerged from these materials was revealing in some respects and disgusting in others.

The purpose of the psychological report was to "illuminate why this middle-aged man with no previous criminal record"—meaning he hadn't been charged and convicted of murder, or any crime for that matter to my knowledge—"would suddenly commit such a serious crime"—meaning kidnapping.

The bottom line was that Conte lacked a father figure in his life—his biological father abandoned him when he was a toddler and subsequent stepfathers were "cold, uncaring and distant"—prompting the young Conte to resort to fantasy to create an "idealized father figure to emulate," an obsession that continued unabated into adulthood. To complicate matters, his mother "sacrificed" his emotional needs "to remain connected to the men she chose."

As a result, Conte erected barriers to closeness and intimacy his entire life, an emotional shield he discarded when he fell head over heels for my mother. And when my mother ended the marriage not long after it started, he snapped because he was unable "to tolerate yet another important figure in his life [walking] away" from him.

The clinical psychologist concluded that the kidnapping effectively was a one-off, a perfect storm convergence of biographical dynamics, and that, as a result, we could all rest assured that Conte did "not pose significant risk of re-offense behavior in the future." Closer to home, he added that Conte did "not pose imminent threat to Ms. Elliott or her family."

The letters of support mostly came from professional colleagues. A few were authored by friends and one by his mother. Each seemed heartfelt, and each described a man I'd never met. Virtually none showed compassion for my mother or our family, but I suppose that was to be expected in the circumstances. One woman, however, in passing, accused my mother falsely of "infidelity." I didn't see how that cheap shot was appropriate.

The letters in one form of another extolled Conte's admirable human qualities—how compassionate and caring he was, how he was so gentle with women and children, and how much of an asset he was to the community. They urged the Court to show him "mercy" because his "bizarre behavior" was "completely atypical of him," he posed "no threat to society," and, in any event, "two days" of misbehavior "should not wipe out an entire life." And, as his mother put it, Conte was a "model son."

But my favorite misstatement was this: "I know that, based on my degree in criminology and my extensive background in law enforcement, this is a one-time type of crime, a crime of passion."

Two months later, on February 25, 2003, the Court held a sentencing hearing. The judge accepted the prosecution's recommendation of concurrent sentences, sparing Conte the prospect of staying in jail potentially into his seventies on the current charges. The Court sentenced him to fifteen years with minimum parole eligibility of six years on the modified kidnapping charge and six years on the administering a controlled substance charge with minimum parole eligibility of twenty-eight months. He received credit for time served— two hundred forty-three days. He was fined $20,000 (ten each for the two counts).

The bottom line: Conte would serve between six and fifteen years. It was still a substantial sentence, and I had to think Conte's evasiveness at the plea agreement hearing factored into the sentencing decision. After all, he didn't exactly own up to his nefarious behavior or, for that matter, show any remorse or empathy toward his victim.

I felt safe, or safer I should say. Conte was going away for a long time. At least it seemed like a long time. I felt almost normal for the first time in many months. Even though I had gotten married in October, I felt I was still on wobbly ground until this point. The conclusion of the kidnapping case was satisfying and gave me optimism. Sure, it was bittersweet. It came with a price. But things were looking up finally. Perhaps the criminal justice system worked the way it was designed to work. Maybe.

The focus now was on getting homicide charges brought in Arkansas and potential sexual assault charges in Utah. I was hopeful that the combination of those hideous felonies would guarantee that Conte would never set foot on free soil again, thus putting him out of our lives forever and making humanity safer.

My newfound faith in justice was about to get throttled.

13

I DIDN'T GIVE IT A second thought. I expected Utah prosecutors to bring sexual assault charges against Conte as a matter of course. Conte had delivered prosecutors the crime essentials on a silver platter. During the initial interview with the DCSO, on June 21, the night of his kidnapping arrest, Conte had admitted to sexual intercourse with my mother, claiming it was consensual. In fact, he boasted about the prolonged duration of their sex act, giving due credit to the Viagra he ingested to boost him along. My mother, drugged for hours on end, had no memory of having sex with him during her entire time in captivity. But no matter, he twice admitted it happened.

He also pled guilty to administering a controlled substance to her, strong enough to knock her unconscious and out of commission for several hours. He told investigators he and my mom didn't leave Salt Lake City for Nevada until 3:30 a.m. on June 21, which meant they were in the condo for close to ten hours. My mother recalled none of that time, save the initial nightmare when she came home to find an armed Conte lying in wait. Hours later she had awakened in the bed of a truck barreling down an interstate highway amid darkness.

What does that say about her consent to what happened in the condo? Could there be any rational doubt that the sex to which

Conte brazenly admitted wasn't consensual? Even if she were half-awake, is there any question everything she did in his presence was compelled under threat of bodily harm and under the influence of Conte's twisted version of a date drug?

There was more.

When my mother began to clear cobwebs from her head, she noticed she wasn't wearing any bra or panties. When investigators asked Conte about it, he said my mother removed them to take a shower with him and, for some unstated reason, didn't put them back on after the shower. So what happened to the undergarments? Conte brought them to Nevada as keepsakes. Putting aside how creepy that is, the removal of her bra and panties, another part of the evening my drugged mother didn't recall, was a stirring piece of inculpatory evidence.

My mother also recounted to investigators that at some point while held prisoner in the cabin in Nevada, she noticed her work scrubs were on backwards. How did that happen? Did she remove the top to voluntarily take the shower? Or, again, did *he* remove her scrub top as part of his efforts to undress my unconscious mother before he did what he'd admitted to doing.

Here is the scenario that rang truest to me. While she was passed out in Salt Lake City, Conte removed her clothes, had sex with her as she lay in a stupor or entirely unconscious, and when he was done, clumsily put the scrubs back on to clothe her for the Nevada journey, and grabbed the bra and panties as souvenirs. Doubtless his fingerprints were all over each of the three items.

The Salt Lake Police had all this information—and still more.

Salt Lake City investigators, in their forensic brilliance, reported without comment that they found no evidence of semen on the bed, as if it was a dispositive conclusion. Really? Had they forgotten their own discovery, at my insistence, that my mother's bed was unmade and ruffled, and the pillowcases and the top sheet were washed and in the dryer dripping wet? Did they forget what I told them repeatedly:

that my mother never leaves the house in the morning unless the bed is made, a routine akin to night following day? Isn't it highly likely that Conte committed sexual assault and washed the bedding to destroy whatever incriminating evidence it contained, rendering the absence of semen *consistent* with the crime since he admitted to sexual intercourse?

I'm betting a first-year prosecutor, wet behind the ears, armed with a healthy dose of rookie jitters, could make that argument to a jury with persuasive force to spare.

In addition, the Salt Lake City police were quick to note they didn't find any semen in the shower stall either. Well, maybe that's because they didn't shower together—Conte may have lied about the shower—and that what happened occurred on the bed which had been disturbed and used during the time my mother was unconscious.

This all raised a few simple questions. What did crime lab tests show of the undergarments and smock? To what extent were Conte's fingerprints found on those items? Was there indications of semen on any of them? How damning was this evidence?

We will never know. Why? Because, other than testing the condo for semen, Salt Lake City investigators didn't do any forensic work at all.

Further, to the extent Utah prosecutors feared a defense attorney acting for Conte might try to turn a sexual assault trial into a "she-said, he-said" skirmish—which defense counsel are wont to do—wholly aside from the physical evidence and the glaring Conte admissions, was there serious question who would have the upper hand regarding credibility? Would it be the convicted felon, who kidnapped, drugged, and threatened to kill my mother? Or, in contrast, would it be my mother, who got placed in a drug-induced daze, dragged out of her home at gunpoint, and held captive for almost forty-eight hours?

The most shocking part of all, however, is that the Salt Lake City officials terminated their investigation and tossed it in the trash can, not for lack of evidence, or concerns about losing before a jury, or any reason having to do with case merits, but because "another agency [was] prosecuting." For real?

I have no legal training, but even I can see the fundamental distinction between a kidnapping that occurred in two states (Utah and Nevada)—which might compel one jurisdiction to defer to another on a kidnapping charge—and other wrongs that occurred solely in one jurisdiction (Utah). The prosecutorial initiatives of Nevada didn't limit or have any impact on whether Utah could bring charges against Conte for what happened within Salt Lake City borders the evening of June 20 and wee hours of June 21. Only the State of Utah had the jurisdictional power to bring the sexual assault charges.

So, what was the real reason Utah passed on bringing charges? It's hard to know. Their response to public records requests were underwhelming, to put it charitably. The grapevine at the time, however, was that when Conte did whatever he did to my mother, Utah investigators and prosecutors were up to their eyeballs in the headline-grabbing Elizabeth Smart kidnapping and rape case and, as a result, were preoccupied.

In early June 2002, less than three weeks before Conte kidnapped my mother, Brian David Mitchell had kidnapped fourteen-year-old Elizabeth Smart at knifepoint from her home in Salt Lake City and, with the help of his wife, Wanda Barzee, held the poor girl captive for nine months, during which Mitchell made the girl his sex slave. Authorities rescued Smart on March 12, 2003, and six days later, brought charges against Mitchell and Barzee for aggravated kidnapping, aggravated sexual assault, and aggravated burglary (all charges that fit the bill for Conte, it should be noted). Eventually, Barzee got sentenced to fifteen years in prison, served time, and got released in 2018 at the age of seventy-two. Mitchell is serving two life sentences.

Taking nothing away from the horror and importance of the Smart case—what happened to that young girl was sickening and I applaud the investigative work—it is hard to fathom that law enforcement personnel in Salt Lake City couldn't spare the minimal resources needed to round out the case for similar charges against

Conte that the State of Nevada had largely built for them. How much more work did they need to put it all together? They pretty much had what they needed to forge ahead, save perhaps a few discreet follow-up investigative queries.

The fact is, they punted. They punted because my mother's victimization didn't register high enough on their priority list. I now know more than I care to know about prosecutorial discretion in bringing charges. But Salt Lake officials turned their backs on my mom when they had a strong case. Their failure to act opened the door for Conte to walk free at some point and do it again, a fear that came home to roost later. And they did so, in my view, in a cowardly way, hiding behind the jurisdiction of another state that didn't have the power to file the charges. It was, to my layperson's thinking, a gross dereliction of duty.

Perhaps because she was unconscious when Conte ran amok in her condo, my mother was spared the memory of what that beast did to her and didn't suffer the depth of trauma that commonly attaches to such disgusting crimes. She never talked about it and seemed to move on. I am grateful for that.

But that my mother may have escaped the ruinous pain others victimized the same way suffer doesn't justify the failure to prosecute. It doesn't excuse Salt Lake City authorities from doing their job. And it sure as hell doesn't help build trust in the criminal justice system and respect for the protective role it is supposed to play in our lives. The decision of the State of Utah to abandon my mother was wrong and shameful. I felt whipsawed and bewildered and angry.

I fell back on reminding myself that Nevada did put Conte away for at least six years and hopefully much longer. I knew, too, that his incarceration could extend for the balance of his natural life, once the Faulkner County head prosecutor, H.G. Foster, brought murder charges against Conte in Arkansas. While pissed off about what went down in Salt Lake City, I clung to the expectation that Mr. Foster would soon take action to protect us for all time from Conte.

My understanding was that investigators shared my expectations and believed, as I did, that Conte killed my father and Timmy Wayne. Once they focused on him and collected evidence, they didn't waver. They felt they had the right guy and, like us, awaited criminal charges.

But not everyone shared that view. I dismissed the contrary views of random people in Conway who made unsolicited remarks to me from time to time that Conte didn't do it, that my father was the victim of a drug deal gone bad or the random act of a local jealous lover who my father might have embarrassed or insulted. I didn't pay them any mind. What did they know?

Much more bothersome, however, were contrary perspectives of family members. My mother, of all people, didn't think Conte killed my father. Her refusal to see what I thought so obvious mystified me. What do they say about victims protecting their abusers? Was my mother trapped in a twisted psychological maze?

Or, I wondered, was something more perverse afoot? Did she and Conte have discussions that led to the murders? What did phone records show about contact between them in April and May? What about emails? I wasn't proud of those thoughts and, happily, they were too far off the charts for me to dwell on, but investigators took a look at the evidence to test the crazy theory. For a short while at least, my mother was on the investigative radar.

I thought it more likely that my mother harbored guilt about what happened to my father and Timmy Wayne. Perhaps she thought she had a hand in driving Conte to romantic insanity to where he took the life of the person he saw blocking his reclamation project.

During the marriage, my mother had drenched Conte in repeated, sometimes daily, notes dripping with expressions of undying love and devotion. The first time she wrote to say she loved him, she followed with, "Yes, it is now in writing. I'm glad." From there, she showered him with amorous turns of phrase like, "Every day with you my heart is a good day," "I miss you and can't wait to kiss your sweet lips," "I dream about you," and "How could you be so creative, thoughtful, generous and absolutely SEXY all in one package?" And she underscored her perpetual loyalty to him, with affirmations like, "I will be the best wife I can be," "You're my love forever," "I want you in my life forever," and "I will spend the rest of my life trying to make you happy."

The record shows that she uttered words of love constantly, referring to the two of them as "soulmates," and telling him, "I love you very much," "Know that I love you," "You're my love," "I miss you lots and lots and lots," "Life without you is empty," and the ultimate, "I need you in my life."

The zinger was penned on January 11, 2002, five weeks before my mother dropped the curtain on the marriage, when she wrote Conte:

"Guess who??? It's your secret lover!!!! It's your soulmate and your best friend!!!!!!!!! Your WIFE! I am in love with you, hottie. Can't wait. Love, Lark." It bears repeating: five weeks before dropping the bomb.

It was easy for me to see that dousing Conte with love proclamations normally reserved for Victorian novels was playing with fire. He was vulnerable and she held power over him, so she could easily harbor guilt about playing him the fool and driving him to the brink of homicidal madness.

I hated having such negative thoughts. I didn't want to think so ill of my mother. I wanted everything to be right with the world and the whole damn thing to go away. But one thing I was learning. You have whatever thoughts come your way and you accept them as real, try to understand them, and deal with them the best you can. Maybe they'll pass or maybe they'll find a long-term resting place. Either way, I wasn't going to hide from the darkest of them. I would take them on whenever and however they appeared.

I hoped these thoughts would pass. It became complicated when Mom's brother Richard Gathright, her sister and brother-in-law Gaye and Kevin Clark, shared her view about Conte. They apparently were resolute: Conte didn't do it. He couldn't have. He did something bad with the kidnapping, that much they conceded, but he didn't commit murder, no way. Someone else did. And they knew him best of all of us.

When people around you have unequivocal faith in a contrary perspective, you naturally begin to question your own. I had to ask myself, *was I missing something? Was Conte too obvious a suspect?* I had seen enough TV and movies to know that the crime narrative can be deceptive, and what it projects at one stage isn't always how the story ends. So I wondered: was it simply too impractical for Conte to drive almost two full days between Utah and Arkansas within the confines of a weekend to pull it off? How could he stay awake the whole time?

And maybe local investigators were too anxious to have a prime suspect after a frustrating month of dead ends. Maybe they pounced too quickly. Maybe the kidnapping, as some letters to the Court in Nevada implored, was truly a "one-off."

Naysayers argued that Conte didn't have a motive. My mother and her brother Richard Gathright specifically told investigators they thought Conte had no reason to kill my father.

On the other hand, I am sure Conte feared my parents might reconnect, burying any chance he had to reignite his failed relationship with my mother. The FBI suspected he'd surveilled them as they partied at my engagement party. If he had spied on them, what other reason would he have had? What better way for a suitor to gather intelligence on a romantic competitor and thus handicap the odds of winning the prize.

In addition to objective signs of a romantic resurgence between my parents, investigators learned that my mother reportedly told a nurse who worked with Conte that, "If anything ever happens between Dick and me, I'm going back to my ex-husband in Arkansas, because we're getting along better now than we ever have." And the nurse apparently told Conte. My mother's comment easily could have been off the cuff, but I doubt Conte received it that way. He was channeling everything through the painful lens of estrangement.

As I tortured myself with these thoughts, I learned that Conte had floated two alibis. The first was that his primary means of transportation, a diesel truck, was disabled the weekend of the murders. He'd had the truck towed May 20 to Lunt Motors, near Duck Creek, for servicing.

The second was in the person of seventy-five-year-old William Pringle, a neighbor and longstanding friend of Conte's who had sold him six parcels of real estate over the years. Pringle told investigators, straight up, that Conte couldn't be the perpetrator because Pringle saw Conte driving his truck that weekend, before it was towed for clutch repair.

I refused to believe any of it. I couldn't imagine that the alibis would stymie the investigation. But I struggled to see straight. I didn't know how this worked. I remained extremely eager. I champed at the bit for news of murder charges. I figured once that happened, we'd be off to the races.

14

WEEKS PASSED WITH NO ACTION. Then months. We found ourselves approaching 2004 with zero indication of charges getting filed. The prosecutor's office had gone radio silent. We felt like orphaned victims. I didn't know what to make of it. It was new territory. Trey and I were frustrated. For virtually everyone else I suppose, the situation was probably "out of sight, out of mind." We lacked that luxury. Even though I had a life and a new husband, and the recent kidnapping insanity was fading in the rearview mirror, obtaining justice for my father's death was essential to my life.

While no expert, I knew murder cases that languished without charges often ended up in the cold case files. As each day passed with no prosecutorial action, the murders of my father and Timmy Wayne vied for a resting place in the annals of unsolved crimes. Evidentiary trails wither. Memories dim. There are those who want to forget, those who'd rather not remember certain things. Our tragedy easily could become old news.

Heckling me were visions of Conte making parole on the kidnapping charges and getting sprung free. But it wasn't something to get exercised about yet. It was early in his prison sentence. But that haunting reality, I feared, could be upon us before we realized it, and then where would we be? What would we do?

The prosecutorial inaction gnawed at me. I began to experience surges of panic. We had to try something. Sitting idle wasn't helping.

Trey and I approached the family attorney, William Clay Brazil. We were unaccustomed to dealing with attorneys, but Brazil made us feel welcome. He had long been a family friend. He empathized with our frustration and said the inertia puzzled him as well. We asked him what could be done. We were beginning to feel helpless and ignored. He said he'd tried to light a fire under head prosecutor, H.G. Foster, once his deputy prosecutor.

On January 8, 2004, Brazil pitched a letter to Foster. He inquired whether he had "any plans to file [charges] in the distant future or if there is an additional information" Foster wanted before acting. Brazil pointed out that the family was "frustrated because the police, including the state, local and FBI," have said "they have enough proof" to charge Conte.

Foster responded three weeks later, on January 27. He first noted that he felt the death of my father "in a personal way, more than most of the homicides that I have investigated and prosecuted." He also claimed he was "aware of all evidence that we have in the case."

Then he dropped a bomb.

"I do not believe that we have enough evidence to give us a snowflake's chance in August of obtaining a conviction," despite adding, "I think that we all know who did it." That phrase, "snowflake's chance in August," would torment me. I have never forgotten it.

Foster didn't stop there. He boldly "guaranteed" that if he filed charges against Conte, the case would never see the light of day before a jury. Why? Because no judge would let that happen. According to Foster, the case wouldn't even survive a probable cause hearing, the early judicial test to determine whether prosecutors have the minimal evidence to justify filing the action in the first place. And, if by some marvel the case survived a probable cause hearing, Foster assured us, it would get bounced on motion for a directed verdict, after prosecutors rested their case, and before the jurors got to deliberate. In either case, he guaranteed the case was so weak, no judge would let jurors get their hands on it to render a verdict.

I was flabbergasted. I realized I didn't have the training to claim I knew better, even though in my heart of hearts I felt I knew the truth. If it were me and my brother alone, two victims irrationally crying out for justice no matter what the state of the evidence, I could understand. But that wasn't the case. Based on what I was told, the entire investigative ensemble—local, state and federal experienced professionals with the most intimate knowledge of the evidence, who had devoted themselves tirelessly to getting at the truth—thought otherwise.

So did, apparently, a panel of FBI agents unconnected to the case. The FBI had asked lead investigator, Sgt. Jim Barrett, to present the case as a teaching tool at a conference before a panel of FBI profilers, who perform probability analyses on the psychological and behavioral profiles of criminals. After a three-hour presentation, the profiler panel couldn't understand why charges had not been filed.

It seemed to me that Foster was in a distinct minority. But he held the levers of power.

Foster rubbed it in a little in the letter by adding that if he charged Conte and lost, Conte would be quick to "brag to everyone on *60 Minutes*, *Prime Time* and in every magazine across the country how he traveled to Conway, murdered Carter Elliott and his friend, and had gotten away with it. And I believe that is exactly what would happen."

But of course, the prospects of that happening had to be weighed. We sure as hell couldn't have H.G. Foster publicly embarrassed, could we?

Foster thought we needed a miracle, like a credible jailhouse confession. For him, the only way charging Conte made sense was if, while serving time for kidnapping, Conte started "talking and bragging about pulling off the homicide." Otherwise, he didn't see the prospects of getting a conviction.

Foster seemingly had given up before he started.

Foster also took a shot at local, state and FBI investigators for having the gall to tell our family there is "enough proof to justify charges being filed. This gets the heat off of them and puts it on me and quite frankly, makes me angry."

Incredible. The head of criminal prosecutions for the good people of Conway, among others, was riled because of pressure to do his job. Of all the comments in the letter, this one concerned me the most. Foster seemed to have lost sight of why the community elected him to the position of head prosecutor. He seemed more concerned with his personal sensibilities and job pressure than fearlessly discharging his duties as a public servant. It didn't augur well.

When I saw the Foster letter I didn't scream and throw anything, as tempting as both impulses felt. I was speechless. Stunned, more like it. It struck me that Foster was content to do nothing. Forever. Sure, if Conte coughed up a provable confession, Foster would leap from behind his desk, wave a flag, and rally the troops. What prosecutor wouldn't? I suspect it doesn't take much daring in that circumstance to answer the call of duty. But in the absence of Conte enthusiastically hoisting a white flag from his Nevada prison cell for the whole world to see, so long as Foster called the shots, it seemed game over.

I wondered whether the prosecutor's office had bounced around these questions. What if Conte doesn't confess? Does that mean they'd never file charges against the man they believed did it? What if Conte did his time or got paroled and began walking the streets again? How would they protect us? Would they give a shit? Even if they brought charges after Conte got released from prison, would they be able to overcome the defense argument that was sure to follow, that too much time had elapsed to hold a fair trial? And if the case proceeded, how much harder would it be to get a conviction because of the passage of several years?

I felt trapped, like I was in a dark windowless locked room with no exit. How long would we be at the mercy of uncertainty? When would it end?

I flashed back to how I felt at the time of the kidnapping, and the despair I felt that I might live the rest of my life under a constant dark cloud. If every prosecutor down the line thought like Foster, it was probable that charges would never be filed. We'd never have our day in court and never taste justice. Conte would go free while we'd have our own life sentence of suffering. The more I thought about it, the more dispirited I became.

Did the inaction have anything to do with politics or professional relationships? Isn't that a fair question to ask?

Recall that David Clark, a deputy prosecutor, was a close friend of my father. They partied and drank together. They hung out together often. They were running buddies.

Recall, too, that in the early morning hours of May 18, after my father and Timmy Wayne hooked up with three women at a bar, one of them evidently married, Clark joined them to carouse. Clark also came by the Shady Valley house later that day, several hours before the killings, to borrow the Detco pressure washer and, after taking the washer home in my father's Jeep, left his car at the property overnight. When police arrived in response to the 911 call the early evening of May 19, they initially thought Clark might be the second victim, a concern that I understand led to frantic calls to Foster. Questions started getting asked about why Clark's car was there and whether he had any connection with the homicides.

When investigators began talking to potential witnesses, they learned that Clark and my father often hung out at the Supper Club in Conway, where I understand illegal gambling took place among some patrons. Investigators expended considerable effort in the first weeks of the investigation drilling down on gambling as a possible motive for the murders, and as they did, Clark's name cropped up here and there. Not a good look for a young local prosecutor.

It raised at least the question whether Clark may have used the power of the prosecutorial office to intercede on behalf of my father in non-criminal legal matters when people owed my father money.

According to investigative files, Clark told money obligors they risked criminal charges for theft if they didn't honor their debts to my father. And, sure enough, in the bat of an eyelash, the debts got paid. In fact, my father included David Clark among his "Favorites" in his cell phone, identifying him as "My Prosecutor." To my knowledge, he was never asked about this and surely would deny it. But having your own personal prosecutor at your beck and call can be a tempting asset to pocket. And while it never happened to my knowledge, I am guessing a professional ethics investigation could ruffle a few feathers.

In addition, recall that another focus of the early investigative effort was the possibility that a jealous husband or boyfriend might be responsible for the killings. Who was with my father when Dad may have incited an offended lover or two? Who knew about them? David Clark had to be on the short list of likely witnesses.

You didn't need a law degree to envision how defense counsel might make hay with this information, if it were credible. I could easily imagine a defense lawyer salivating at the possibility to showcase that David Clark may have witnessed illegal gambling while engaged in socializing, and performed a reputed role as private *consigliere* of debt collection for my father. None had to be true or central, only tantalizing enough to create diversions and doubt in the courtroom and serve as grist for the media mill. Whether it would have any appreciable impact on guilt or innocence was beside the point. It could put Foster on the defensive and embarrass him.

The head prosecutor is a political position. My father's case was apparently the first twin homicide in Conway's history, and my father was a prominent businessman in a small community. The combo guaranteed that the criminal case would be subject to sharp local scrutiny. Foster could ill afford to have defense counsel, or the media, fan flames of how deputy prosecutors may have either used the town as their personal playpen, turned a blind eye to illegal conduct, or misused the power of the office. If the trial judge opened the gates to evidence of those matters, Foster's reputation, and his political standing, easily could get soiled. As a political animal, it's last thing he'd want to have happen.

Did political pretext drive Foster's refusal to bring charges? As someone on the outside, I couldn't be sure. But it wouldn't surprise me. Conway was a small Southern community. It had a well-entrenched "good ol' boy" network, where folks were expected to have each others' backs. In certain circumstances, that loyalty is admirable. In others, where public service is concerned, it can be troubling. And where the heart of criminal justice is at stake, its possibility seemed to my layperson's mind nothing but entirely inappropriate?

Was Foster guilty of selling his prosecutorial discretion to finance his political future? Was he refusing to proceed with my father's case, in part or entirely, for political reasons? I didn't know the answers. But the chance alone produced a rancid stench.

No doubt Foster would deny politics had anything to do with his adamant refusal to act, and maybe that was true. But from my standpoint, as the daughter of a murdered father, the mere possibility that a political agenda might have shaped the decision of a prosecutor not to bring criminal charges against someone he acknowledged "we all [knew]" did it, was hugely bothersome.

Whatever actual motivations, Foster wouldn't budge. He was stuck on the perspective that the circumstantial evidence investigators assembled and believed was more than sufficient to move forward wasn't good enough for him.

Someone apparently suggested a strategy at one point to Foster to get him off the dime. They suggested that if he brought capital murder charges against Conte and announced he was seeking the death penalty, Conte would likely plead out in a nanosecond to avoid capital punishment. Conte would, the thinking went, effectively confess. The strategy was simple: charge and arrest and see what happens. If it played out as envisioned, the criminal case would be done in months, without the burden, angst, expense, and risks of a trial.

It made sense. Conte wouldn't take that risk. He was, in the deeper recesses of his being, an insecure, afraid little boy, a banty rooster who lived life as a big lie, propagating fantasy after fantasy to prop himself up for the world around him to see. He stood on fragile underfooting.

I was told Foster wasn't persuaded. He was having none of that sort of thing. He wasn't bringing charges so long as he was head dog in the office, and that was that, unless and until Conte bared his soul first.

It was clear that our prospects for justice hinged on Foster's tenure as head prosecutor coming to an end. If and until that happened, we were in limbo and powerless. All we could do was pray for a changing of the guard.

15

FEELING LIKE A VICTIM OF the system and the crime, I was tempted to indulge in occasional bouts of self-pity, the kind that asks, "Why me, God?" Feeling persecuted could be a useful distraction from anger and frustration. So, rather than bang my head against the wall each day about Foster's refusal to act, I presumed God had dealt me one of life's shitty hands, and it was simply my personal cross to bear.

My parents' divorce had taught me early that our little worlds can change quickly and thrust us on unfamiliar paths. I had a certain life one day, and the next day quite a different one. It was how the world worked. You adjusted and reset expectations.

When my father was murdered, however, at age 48, when I was a raw and spirited 25, my soul got so throttled that adjustments and new expectations didn't come easily. They weren't part of any emotional playbook my father had left behind or my mother was equipped to provide. It wasn't simply a life directional change. Instead, my entire psychic universe got reordered. Horizons shifted. Everything I saw, felt, and did got filtered through the eyes of a traumatized victim desperately trying to cope with hopelessness. The sun rarely reached my heart. I was in constant emotional survival mode, holding on tight so I didn't completely lose my shit.

The kidnapping escapade pushed me much closer to the edge. It was a cruel bitch slap that sent my entire being spinning off its axis for weeks. Once the ordeal passed, I saw a pattern, a series of punishments for family sins. Life had become scarily unpredictable, a rollercoaster ride of "Okay, what's next?" Paranoia dropped into the driver's seat.

I craved a steady diet of feel-good reliability. Not something as common as the sun rising each day, but more specific to me, down on the ground, like a steady string of routines that played out as designed or uplifting events like the impending birth of a child or a wedding anniversary I couldn't wait to celebrate. My capacity for upheaval had deflated until it was to close to none.

So I am glad I didn't learn until much later what happened next in the criminal investigation. It would have accelerated me into insanity.

In late July 2005, more than three years after the murders, lead investigator Sgt. Jim Barrett got a call from Rob Conway, a retired member of the Arkansas State Police (ASP). Conway told Barrett he had gotten a call from a woman who told him, "we know who killed Carter Elliott." The caller added, "Tommy Morrison is the one who killed Carter Elliott."

Tommy Morrison was a familiar name to the general public. Born in Arkansas, he became a professional prizefighter and once held a heavyweight title, taking it away from legendary George Foreman. After an eight-year career, he was suspended from boxing after testing positive for HIV. In his heyday, Morrison starred in *Rocky V* alongside "Sly" Stallone.

Tommy Morrison wasn't a stranger to law enforcement. After his forced retirement from boxing, he cascaded downward, piling up a long rap sheet including arrests for assault, public intoxication, DWI, and illegal possession of firearms.

Conway referred Barrett to current ASP officers who had experience with Morrison. Barrett learned that the former boxer was erratic, considered a "violent person" and known to possess "multiple guns" and "ammunition."

Barrett tracked down the initial caller, Wanda Fincher, who had worked on Morrison's autobiography. Fincher said my father and Alan Duke and Morrison had often hung out at a sports bar in Little Rock, and the three had worked on promoting a local boxing match involving a middleweight prospect. She added that rumors had Morrison with mob connections.

The story went that for uncertain reasons, the promotion deal the three cooked up went sideways and gushed bad blood. At the time, Morrison had fallen on bad financial times and was, according to Fincher, "dead broke, I mean broke," and confided in her that if he got desperate, he'd take up work as a hit man. After my father was killed, according to Fincher, Morrison became flush with cash and went on a "wild" spending spree.

Investigators found no tangible evidence to tie Morrison to what happened at Shady Valley. As best they could tell, Morrison likely was in Oklahoma at the time, recently married, and rebuilding his life after serving a prison term. Barrett determined that the lead ran its course.

Investigators had always been up-front with me. Sgt. Barrett made it clear he would always tell me the truth, but making sure to point out he couldn't share everything. The important thing was that I felt I could always rely on him. I felt safe with him.

I was grateful Sgt. Barrett kept me in the dark about the Morrison lead. While he had to run it down, he probably suspected it had no traction. Telling me would have thrown more confusion and anxiety into the mix at a time when I was desperate for clarity and needed normalcy in my life. By then, I was trying tried to redirect my energy to life's basics, pushing to the back of my mind any possibility of charges being brought. I hadn't given up, not by a long shot, but I had begun to yield to time's natural way of reformulating expectations. Too much hope, I was learning, can be an unkind trap.

As 2006 approached, miracle of miracles, we got word that H.G. Foster was moving on, leaving the office of head prosecutor for a more powerful and visible prosecutorial role at the state level. There would be a new sheriff in town. Praise be to God. We eagerly awaited the next round of state and county elections with the renewed expectation that, when Foster's successor picked up the mantle of head prosecutor, criminal charges would soon follow. Hope sprang eternal again on our rollercoaster ride.

Soon after the Foster announcement, Marcus Vaden, Foster's chief deputy, announced his candidacy to succeed him. And, as it turned out, he would run unopposed. I took no comfort in Vaden stepping into Foster's shoes. He was a member of the "good ol' boys" network in Conway and I assumed was intimately involved in evaluating my father's case with Foster. Of course, that he may have supported the Foster non-action position didn't necessarily mean he agreed. It was possible, at least, that he played yes-man to the boss, keeping his differing views close to the vest. And while I knew enough to pause my excitement, the door had cracked open, allowing a shred of light into the room. Would Vaden fling the door open wide and walk in or slam it shut on our fragile fingers?

Vaden took office at the turn of 2007. We gave him some time to adjust to his office. We waited, first with patience, then with eager anticipation, and then with rising annoyance. We placed unreturned calls. I eventually got him on the phone and complained about the lack of communication and action. I said, "If you could just pick up the phone and say, 'I don't have any new information. We are still working on it.' Anything of that nature, I would really appreciate it." His response was something along the lines of: "Yeah, yeah. Well, there's just so much stuff to go through. You know, I've got, like, eleven boxes."

My mother, I am told, showed up at his office one early morning, unscheduled, and insisted on speaking to him. She waited hours. Vaden didn't emerge, leaving her to stew. Frustrated, she finally left. At least Foster humored us. He wrote a letter.

On March 22, 2008, coming on six years after the murders, William Pringle, the alibi witness for Conte who'd put Conte in Utah at the time of the murders and had risen to become the linchpin of the Conte defense, passed away. Not relishing Mr. Pringle's death, we were nonetheless elated that a key part of the defense strategy had dissolved to dust.

Your move, Mr. Vaden.

Vaden still wouldn't bring charges. Once again, I was stunned. Maybe the whispers about a domineering political agenda had a ring of truth.

I knew how powerless feels, like when Conte held my mother captive while we frantically tried to dissuade him from killing her from hundreds of miles away. It is a frightening place to be, to see any chance of what you urgently need to happen steadily evaporate in the hands of another. I felt trapped in a political system that didn't seem to care a whit about us as crime victims. I struggled to find continued purpose. I kept close to my heart the fact that Daddy would have never given up on finding my killer. He would have gone to the ends of the earth to get justice for his little girl. I wasn't about to let him down. I could almost hear my father cheering me on, urging me to keep up the good fight for him.

"Don't give up, let up, or shut up," he would have said.

Vaden's first term of office ran through 2010. Perhaps, I thought, we should get involved in the election. To my way of thinking, politics had become the driver. Much as I hated the idea, we had to consider whether we could influence the politics of the situation to eliminate the stalemate. It was worth considering.

In the meantime, we had a matter on the front burner. We had to do what we could to keep Conte in jail as long as possible.

Shortly after Mr. Pringle passed away, we received word that Nevada authorities had scheduled Conte's first parole hearing for June 17, 2008. My mother and I made plans to attend and participate to the extent allowed.

As the hearing approached, I became super anxious. Although we had received general instructions about what to expect, it was hard to know what the experience would be like. When the day arrived and we entered the prison facility, I found myself managing a rough sea of emotions. I was nervous and intimidated. I was also afraid, not physically, but emotionally. I was afraid about what I might feel once the hearing started. I was afraid how I'd react when I cast my eyes on Conte. Would I lose it? I immersed myself in a steady monologue to keep it together, telling myself all would be fine. We'll get through this okay. We're doing the right thing.

When we got inside the hearing area, we were told we wouldn't be in the same room with Conte. He would be on video and we could watch him on a monitor screen. From where we sat, he couldn't see us. That was fine with me.

Interestingly, he came out in a wheelchair, apparently because he had developed multiple sclerosis and had paralysis on his left side. He also had vision difficulty in one eye. The skeptic that I was, I had doubts about the wheelchair. Conte had, to my way of thinking, pulled wool over some eyes. I saw the wheelchair as a theatrical prop. His latest manipulative fantasy.

Seeing him inflamed my anger, bringing back all the fury. I broke out into a sweat. I wanted to beat him. I wanted to scream at him. I wanted to jump through the telemonitor and throw him down. I felt sick and disgusted and wasn't sure I'd make it through the hearing. It was a tough few minutes before I restrained my pounding heart.

Conte pitched his case. He pleaded with the parole board to grant an immediate release so he could live out his remaining days with his mother in Wisconsin. He made it sound as if he was on his death bed. He claimed he was currently incapable of doing harm to anyone, including my mother. In his condition he wasn't a threat to anyone other than—and he actually said this—"rolling over" my mother's toes with his wheelchair. I guess he thought tongue-in-cheek advocacy might work. No one laughed.

I recall two people speaking on his behalf: his ninety-five-year-old mother, and his friend and former medical colleague, George Alexander. Both had written letters in early 2003 for the Court to consider in the sentencing phase of the kidnapping case.

Alexander said the kidnapping "shouldn't have happened"—evidently, what Alexander deemed a generous concession—and he offered the imaginative (and unsubstantiated) opinion that an undiagnosed and advancing multiple sclerosis condition may have "triggered" the kidnapping misbehavior. He boldly finished with, "The time he's served should be sufficient now." Because of public knowledge, I assumed Alexander knew Conte was the prime suspect in the murders of my father and Timmy Wayne when he made those comments.

When her turn came, Conte's mother got too choked up to read a prepared statement, and asked someone to read it for her. She urged "a compassionate release" for her son. She also wanted mercy for herself. She lamented that, in the absence of a release now, she might live her final days apart from him, still incarcerated. She said he was her "only living child"—her daughter had died several months ago—and closed with "I beg you for a favorable release." Even though the poor woman was ninety-five, I struggled to empathize with her. Her son murdered my father as far as I was concerned, and he kidnapped my mother, too. Where was his compassion? And where, I thought, was yours toward us?

My mother and I both voiced our opposition. We told the board we considered Conte dangerous and a risk to hurt our family members again. We urged the panel to keep him in prison the full term of his sentence. At one point, I asked to address him directly.

I changed my seat to face the camera so he could see me. My body shook as if I had uncontrollable fever chills. I couldn't stop shaking. It wasn't fear. It was the accumulation of what I had suffered at his hands—the murders, kidnapping, and betrayal. I managed to speak.

"I want to know why you did this to me? You took my trust and ripped it apart." I stated.

Keeping his head down, he said, "I was trying to revive and rekindle a relationship that I know now was not there."

"You've ripped my life apart," I responded. "I trusted you. I trusted you with my mother."

"I didn't mean in any way to injure you either emotionally or physically." His words and tone seemed scripted. I realized that dealing with him in this setting was futile. I held back going after him about my father. I'd probably make a scene, and it would destroy me inside. I decided to stop. I was still shaking.

Three weeks later Nevada authorities denied Conte parole, sparing us the specter of him as a free man for at least two more years when the next parole hearing would likely happen.

Meanwhile, by all indications, Vaden had dumped my father's case into a cold storage bin. He evidently wasn't going to file charges in the absence of a signed, sealed, and delivered confession. His lack of action said to me that he was comfortable with Conte going free when his time was up. It was beyond mindboggling. The day Conte became free meant that the risk of death would be on my doorstep dressed up as a mercenary killer, taser in one hand, gun with silencer in the other. It was time to focus on a political solution.

The following year, Cody Hiland, a local attorney, announced he intended to challenge Vaden for the top prosecutor position in the upcoming election. Hiland seemed sympathetic to my family's plight. He invited my brother and me to lunch. Hiland said that, if elected, he would actively look into bringing charges against Conte. That was all I needed to hear to support his campaign. I donated my own money, hit up family and friends for more, filmed a supportive video to air on local TV networks, and gave public interviews.

Sometime after I became a public supporter of the Hiland campaign, David Clark spotted me at a party in Conway, and when our eyes met, he came over to see me. He seemed drunk. He wanted to talk about the Hiland campaign. I didn't know what to make of it, so I said nothing, waiting for him to continue. He then said, in a lecturing tone, "You shouldn't have done that. It was a mistake."

I shook my head and walked away. I was appalled.

I didn't get it. Clark was supposed to be a close friend of my father. In fact, Clark told investigators how my father helped him "through a lot of tough times, a lot of personal crises," and here he was, giving me shit for doing what little I could do to get murder charges brought against the person everyone seemed to agree was the killer. I would have thought Clark would lead the charge to make that happen. I would have thought Clark valued his friendship with my father enough to do everything he reasonably could to avenge his death. After all, not only were they running and bosom buddies, but in the eyes of my father, Clark was "My Prosecutor." My poor father had to be turning over and over in his grave.

The next parole hearing occurred in June 2010. My mother and Trey attended for the family. It apparently went the same way as the first hearing. A few weeks later the board again denied parole. Conte would serve the duration of his sentence. Justice on occasion can be teased from the system.

I continued to hope for criminal charges. But I was wearing down. I started to think there might come a time when I'd have to give up the crusade, when I'd have to focus on living the rest of my life without the satisfaction of achieving justice from the legal system. Each day it got harder to see light at the end of the tunnel, and I began for the first time to think that giving up the ghost might be best. Maybe walking away from the fight might free me in a different way. I had heard people talk about restorative justice and how victims forgive their perpetrators. I couldn't imagine ever going there. I didn't think I had it in me to forgive. But I could appreciate the freedom that might come by kicking the pursuit of vengeance to the curb. It had been a heavy emotional burden. It'd be nice to get it off my shoulders.

Giving it up also might allow me to deal better with the ill feelings I had toward my mother's family. The entire awful experience was wrapped up with them—how they hated my father, how they brought Conte in our lives, how they blamed me for this and that, and how I thought they might bear some responsibility, not necessarily legally, but morally, for what happened. I doubted we could reconcile fully. But if I walked away from pursuit of the criminal case, maybe I could bridge some of the gap with family members.

It didn't take me long to realize I had entertained those thoughts too soon.

In August 2010, my mother's family—about ten of us—gathered for a post-wedding dinner at Mr. Chow's restaurant in Manhattan. A cousin had gotten married a few days before, and we were having a private re-celebration of the happy event.

We were well into the dinner when Kevin Clark caught my eye and leaned toward me to speak.

"How's everything going with your Dad's case?" he asked.

I shrugged my shoulders. "Not much. Waiting." I didn't encourage more. It didn't seem like dinner conversation and, regardless, I definitely didn't want to go there.

"You know, I remember us sitting around telling Dick how we thought, you know, everything would be better if your Dad was dead." He didn't laugh or smile. He was serious. My heart dropped into my stomach.

I waited for my mother to run interference and jump all over him, to tell him how inappropriate and mean he was being, to give him the public scolding he deserved. She stayed stone cold silent, leaving me hanging, like the rest of them. No one said a word.

I sat perfectly still trying to keep it together. My eyes began to well with tears. I pushed away from the table and announced I was going to the bathroom. Once there, alone and safely removed from family, I cried my eyes out. I couldn't believe how cruel that was. *What kind of person says that to the daughter of an assassinated father? What kind of person says people would be better off if my dad was dead? Who thinks like that?*

Later that night, my mother, with whom I was sharing a hotel room, broached the subject. Having had time to think about it, this was the best she could do.

"Ashley, look, your uncle Kevin was drunk. He didn't mean anything by the comment."

Seriously? I thought. *Didn't mean anything?*

"Well, Mom, answer me this; is it true? Did he say those words in front of Conte?"

"Well, yeah, but understand he was joking. They were drinking. You know how your uncle can be and how he and your dad didn't always see eye to eye." She wasn't about to address my feelings, that was clear. She didn't get it.

"When did he say those things?"

"During a family vacation."

"Before Dad was killed?"

"Yes."

I didn't care how drunk he was, then or now. More than eight years had passed since the murders and nothing had been done about it. Was there more truth to learn? I couldn't sit on the information.

When I returned to Arkansas, I called Sgt. Barrett and told him all about the dinner. He said he would pass the information to the FBI, and he apparently did, because the FBI made an unannounced house call to the Clarks in Utah to follow up.

The Clarks were furious with me, as was my mother. They all evidently made it sound like a big joke to the FBI, a huge misunderstanding. I assumed the Clarks denied any involvement in the killings, although I wondered whether they were candid enough to admit they hated my father and didn't want my mom to stay married to him. To this day, I struggle to believe that I have heard everything my mother's family knows about my father's killing, or at least the circumstances leading up to it. And to this day as well, because I am apparently to blame for siccing the FBI on the Clarks to help the investigation into my father's death, I am *persona non grata* in my mother's family.

The Mr. Chow's episode reignited my spirit to stay focused on the criminal process. I was even more buoyed when in November 2010, Cody Hiland was elected to top prosecutor in a landslide. Vaden would soon be out, and the roadblock to criminal charges would soon lift. I was excited and waited for Hiland to bring murder charges against Conte, once he transitioned to the job.

When 2011 arrived, days turned into weeks and weeks turned into months. Before we knew it, the summer was upon us, and still nothing. We were in a familiar a holding pattern. The family began again to get antsy. What was going on? Had I been played?

My mother had been keeping tabs on prison release dates, lobbing regular calls to the Nevada authorities for updates. She was hyper-sensitive about Conte getting free, and kept checking up for assurances. I understood completely and was pleased she stayed on top of it.

On Monday, August 22, 2011, first thing in the morning, she called the same person who had been giving her updates. She was told, "I'm so glad you called. He is being released early, Sunday, August 28."

What!? That was six days away! What happened to the rest of his sentence? We were shocked. Instant panic mode set in.

The next day, August 23, my mother Trey, and I each filed applications for temporary restraining orders to bar Conte from coming anywhere near us or trying to contact us. The Court granted them the same day. We knew the existence of a court order barring Conte from approaching us didn't guarantee our safety. He had shown little respect for the law and we continued to believe he was unhinged. But other than arming ourselves, legal self-help was all we had for the time being. TROs in hand, we braced for what was to come next.

16

CONTE WASN'T GETTING PAROLED. HE wasn't getting chained to a short leash to meander under the long shadow of a watchful parole officer. In prison lingo, he had flattened out his time. He was about to be let out without restriction and become a free-roaming citizen like the rest of us. A moment of reckoning had arrived. If an unconditional Conte release didn't force the prosecutor's hand to bring murder charges, nothing would.

News of the upcoming release broke quickly. On August 25, Thursday, the daily newspaper in Conway, the *Log Cabin Democrat,* published an article titled, "Cold Case May Warm up with Possible Release of Ex-Suspect." The paper noted how the impending release of Conte had me reliving my father's death. I told them:

"This man admitted to kidnapping my mother, and I believe he murdered my father. I'm pleading for me and my family. . . .This situation is looming over us, and it will for the rest of my life. I just want some protection against Conte. . . . I feel like I have to keep trying and get this case resolved. I might fail, but I'd rather fail than not try at all; that is what Dad would want. He wasn't a quitter."

Head prosecutor Cody Hiland weighed in with:

"This is obviously a very extensive file and we've examined it closely over the last few months. We anticipate making a decision in the very near future about whether or not to pursue prosecution."

The words "whether or not to pursue prosecution" jumped off the page at me. I wanted to believe that his words were carefully chosen prosecutor-speak for "I'm not telling you what I am going to do until I do it." I wanted to believe Hiland was cagily keeping intention to file from public scrutiny, including from Dick Conte. Still, his comment was no less ambiguous than a shoulder-shrugged, "maybe, maybe not," a non-committal that didn't square with what I'd thought he had conveyed to my family. In light of the torturous history we endured during two previous prosecutorial tenures, it was hard to stem the tide of anxiety rising inside me that Hiland might also pass on filing charges. I couldn't help but think "here we go again."

And what did he mean by "in the very near future?" Could that extend beyond the few remaining days Conte had left in prison? Would a few days or weeks matter? We did have the TROs, for what they were worth. And what happens once Conte goes to Wisconsin, where I assumed he'd first go? Could he disappear? As crazy as that sounded, with the wheelchair thing, those were my thoughts. My imagination may not have been rooted in rationality, but I had come to expect the worst; I had come to expect the unexpected.

But that didn't last. The key word, it turned out, in "very near future," was "very."

On Friday, the next day, August 26, at 11 a.m., Hiland initiated a series of decisive actions. He first filed two counts of capital murder against Conte. He took immediate steps for the State of Arkansas to seek extradition of Conte from Nevada to face the charges. And he faxed the charges to the Northern Nevada Correctional Center where Conte resided, asking that the prison hold off releasing Conte pending the extradition process.

On news of the charges, I gushed tears mixed with joy, pain, gratitude, and relief. I had had an emotional outpouring like that before.

It consumed and overwhelmed me. I felt the spirit of my father deep within me. "Daddy, we didn't give up. Daddy, we are close." We had waited nine long years for this day. My constant prayers had received a favorable answer. We were getting our day in court. We were getting the chance to avenge the cold-blooded murders of our father and Timmy Wayne. We knew we had not emerged from the tunnel. We knew there was work to do. But for the first time, our eyes fixed upon a bright light beaming at the distant end of that long tunnel, which for almost a decade had kept all light out. We had a legitimate expectation that justice might prevail. Justice wouldn't fix everything. I knew that. It never could. But it was essential and now, within our reach.

August 26, 2011 was the first day of the rest of my life.

Conte resisted extradition, kicking off a legal proceeding in Nevada. It was rare, I learned, for fugitives from justice within the U.S. to resist extradition. Acquiescence in the face of an interstate extradition request normally followed as a matter of course. Did Conte have something up his sleeve? Had he planned for this day? More uncertainty. In the meantime, at the request of Arkansas, Nevada kept him under lock and key at a local jail.

A Nevada judge held two hearings over the course of a month. Conte protested that prison officials had repeatedly told him he was no longer a suspect. He couldn't understand why this was happening. There must be a mistake. He also complained that he couldn't afford an attorney, making the entire process unfair. And his most passionate plea was his medical disability, which he insisted required medical attention unavailable to him in prison but available in Wisconsin. He should be allowed to go home to Wisconsin to live out his dying days.

On September 30, 2011, the judge deemed extradition proper and ordered Conte transferred to Arkansas. I was elated.

Still, visualizing Conte in Arkansas, and the thought of seeing him in a courtroom, induced in me a wave of mixed feelings, as I told *The Cabin Democrat*.

"On the one hand, I am excited because I know why he's here and needs to be held responsible for killing my Dad. On the other hand, I'm overwhelmed. I'm concerned about having to face him. I really don't want to see him, but I am thankful that he will finally stand trial for his actions."

Arkansas authorities dispatched lead investigator (now Lt.) Jim Barrett and a supervisor to Nevada to retrieve Conte. Officials kept the timing of their visit secret from Conte. They harbored concerns he might harm himself if he knew when he'd be snatched. They wanted to surprise him best they could. Barrett had in hand a governor's warrant, a special arrest warrant used to extradite fugitives in another state. Strings were pulled to get Barrett the governor's plane to expedite. And off they went.

Upon their arrival at the jail, the Conway investigators served an unsuspecting Conte with the governor's warrant, making him officially the custody of the State of Arkansas. Barrett secured him with hand restraints and told him they were headed to Arkansas.

Conte was taken aback. He had assumed he wouldn't leave Nevada for a while. "You're taking me back?" was his reaction. He seemed genuinely flabbergasted. Back they went to the plane for takeoff to Arkansas.

It was a long flight back, several hours. Restrained with belly chains and ankle shackles, Conte sat next to Lt. Barrett. During most of the flight, Barrett and Conte engaged in fairly uninterrupted chit-chat about mundane matters, like hunting, life in Nevada, medical facilities in prison, biographical background, and even some joke telling. Every now and then, though, Barrett deftly nudged the discussion near the edges of the murder case, casually floating random open-ended questions.

Barrett asked his prisoner how he felt about the prospects of seeing my family in court. Conte called up the discomfort that led him to "plead guilty to the charges that put me in prison for nine years." That was the same line he peddled to the judge in the sentencing hearing in the kidnapping case: he was pleading guilty to avoid seeing my mother and the rest of us in a courtroom. He then implied his innocence on the kidnapping charges, offering that my mother "had agreed to go with" him to Utah—meaning he hadn't really kidnapped her—and that the situation got out of hand only because while in the truck she suffered a bout of "the DTs" (*delirium tremens*) because of her alleged alcoholism. And it was that, not his use of force, that triggered her resistance. He professed to have the purest of motives for dragging her from Utah to Nevada, essentially describing himself as a savior, a one-person intervention to free my mother from the "bad influence" of "people in Salt Lake," which I assume meant me and my mother's family, as if we were a cult that had latched its evil grips on her.

After nine years, he still hadn't come to terms with the magnitude of what he did to my mother. Perhaps that explained why the Nevada parole board denied his release each time.

When Barrett returned to the subject of his seeing us in court, Conte seemed non-plussed about the prospects. He said he had never "even met Trey," complaining that Trey "didn't come to the wedding." He dismissed me as a "little drama queen," and to illustrate his hostility, complained that at his first parole hearing I "showed up and was carrying on." He sloughed off any concerns about seeing my mother as well, whom he had stopped calling his "estranged wife," dropping the curtain on their history with the definitive barb, "I'm over her."

He revealed that he was "more anxious about seeing my ex-brother-in-law, Kevin Clark, because he was my best friend for twenty-one years." He bitched about how Clark "never" visited him in prison in Nevada and that when he first got arrested, he "sobbed," telling himself, "Oh, he'll come for this." He so wanted Kevin Clark to come see him and felt abandoned when Clark was a perpetual no-show. When Barrett asked him whether he thought Clark turned his back on him because of what he did to my mother, Conte said, "no, it's because of the family."

They eventually got around to talking about my father. Conte said he had "never met" my dad. He only "knew about him" and how my family "hated him." Conte referred to us as "a dysfunctional family" and that we were all "crazy" and said how my grandfather, on my mother's side, "used to say he would kill—oh, what his name?—Carter, if he could get away with it." Twice during the flight he repeated that my mother wanted my father dead and told him "she would kill [my father] with her last dying breath."

Conte explained that my mother resented my father because she got "shafted" in their divorce settlement. As he told it, my father got all the real estate and bulk of their property and she only got some spending money. That had infuriated him, and he hoped to confront my father at my wedding for the financial mistreatment, "if I'd have enough guts."

As Conte gave Barrett his measured description about how my mother wanted my father dead, he didn't hesitate to share thoughts about how the murders may have gone down.

Barrett: "Well, these two murders in Conway: Did you think it's possible that [Lark Elliott] manipulated the person responsible into doing it for her?"

Conte: "Well, she knows people in Conway. I assume that you'd have to have someone that knew Carter to do it."

Barrett: "Why do you think that?"

Conte: "Well, the last I heard, he was in San Francisco. That's what Ashley told me. So you'd have to know he's home and have to get someone to open the door for you."

Barrett: "You don't think a person could have just rang the doorbell and have him answer?"

Conte: "No. I don't know. I never thought about that. I thought it must have been a friend or someone. Lark said they were in the foyer, so [whoever did it had to do] something to get both people in the foyer."

Barrett: "Well, if the person responsible for it was put up to it by Lark, I know she will be held accountable for what she did."

Conte: "Yeah. I don't see how one person could overpower two people."

Barrett: "Well, I reckon it would be possible if the person had a gun and they didn't. A lot of folks will do a lot of things if you've got a gun pointed at them."

Conte: "I think Lark used to say it had been a professional hit. . . . But still, I think that you'd need a friend or someone to ring the bell to get both guys in the foyer."

The trio landed in Arkansas on October 4, 2011, and Conte was brought to the Conway jail. The next day, October 5, Conte made his first court appearance in the Faulkner County Court, and pled not guilty to the charges. The Court set an initial trial date of December 8, 2011, although I understood it likely would be moved by at least a year if not more. Conte requested that the Court appoint him a public defender (PD) and permit him to act as co-counsel. A representative from the Public Defenders Commission told the judge they'd assign a PD within two days. The judge told Conte he could renew his co-counsel request once that happened.

None of that interested me. I was waiting eagerly for what came next. Would the Court deny or set bail? And if the Court set bail, did Conte have the resources to raise what he'd need? I literally was on the edge of my courtroom seat. And then, more good news. The Court directed that Conte be held without bail. He was going nowhere.

I walked out of the courthouse that day with renewed optimism—we were safe—and had clear direction—we were headed for trial.

As we were warned, the trial date got moved. Conte agreed to waive his constitutional right to a "speedy trial" in favor of more time to prepare his defense and, as we were to learn, ample time to seek dismissal of the case. The Court reset trial for January 15, 2013.

On January 18, 2012, Conte filed a motion to dismiss the case on the grounds that prosecutors had delayed too long to file charges. The inaction of Foster and Vaden had come home to roost in a big way. Even though the prosecution told us to expect this motion, truth be known, they seemed worried about it. That made me worry, too, of course, probably much more than they worried. For a layperson, it's one thing to be warned about something like that. It's another to watch from front row seats of a courtroom, as I did, a pitched battle between well-prepared advocates when the future of the case lay in the balance.

Defense counsel—Conte had found the funds to retain a private attorney to replace the appointed PD—pointed out that no eyewitness saw Conte and not "a shred of forensic evidence linked him to the murders." The tenuous nature of Conte's connection to the alleged crimes made the passage of time even more problematic, he asserted, especially since Conte had a credible eyewitness that placed him in Utah the weekend of the murders. The eyewitness put a glaring light on the absence of direct evidence and exposed the prosecutor's case for what it was, a collage of innuendo unworthy of the attention of a jury. The alibi, he argued further, thus gave Conte an air-tight defense, which he'd still have but for the fact that the eyewitness, Mr. William Pringle, died almost six years after the murders. The inexcusable delay at the hands of Foster and Vaden robbed Mr. Conte of a key element of his defense and in the process denied him the fundamental fairness he is entitled to enjoy under the due process clause of the United States Constitution. The argument filled the entire courtroom with persuasion.

Sitting there, under the influence of the advocacy, I started to freak out. I was learning that when skilled attorneys argue with passion, they display an assuredness that draws you to their power and puts you under a spell. But it was more than that. Lassiter's advocacy had a basic logic to it: "You, Mr. Prosecutor, delayed and by doing so, took for yourself a major advantage that my client had. You gamed the system and that wasn't fair."

It made perfect sense. Listening to the defense pound past prosecutorial inaction into the ground over and over sickened me. The lawyer made the additional point that the case had been fully investigated by late 2002 or early 2003. Nothing had changed, except the end of the life of an alibi witness. There was no justifiable reason for the delay.

Of course I agreed. There was no legitimate justification for the delay. Sitting in the courtroom, I became disgusted. Foster and Vaden had rolled the dice, maybe for political reasons, and now my family and justice might pay the ultimate price of having the case bounced. Each defense point sent a dagger deep into my heart. And when Conte's lawyer cited legal authority, including a prior case where an alibi witness had died during a much shorter prosecutorial delay, I became besieged with fright that the Court would grant the motion and Conte would walk.

The prosecutor pushed back. He argued that the delay wasn't designed to gain an advantage, but was due to circumstances they didn't control, an argument that, meaning no disrespect, sounded like bullshit to me. Foster and Vaden totally controlled the circumstances of their decision. I had the H.G. Foster letter, which at that point remained within the family and our attorney. I had no clue it might become important in a formal sense. I knew the prosecutorial history. Apart from any possible political cover, they delayed for strategic advantage as they perceived it. They made a calculated judgment to wait, to improve chances of success, however misguided. And while it was true, as the prosecutor argued, that the investigation was ongoing—by then I knew about the Tommy Morrison dead end lead—that seemed a technicality born of strategic inaction.

Despite its confidence and force, the arguments of the prosecutor seemed inferior. They lacked the passion and punch that allowed defense counsel to invoke the power of the U.S. Constitution and respect for fundamental fairness. I couldn't help but think the defense had the upper hand.

It didn't help when the Court said, "I'd be less than honest if I didn't tell you I was concerned about the delay and the loss of Mr. Pringle." He then took the matter "under submission." He had to think about it.

Despite the up-in-air status of the ruling, I felt defeated. We were going to lose. I walked out of the courtroom with my head down.

On April 26, in a letter barely more than one page long, much to my surprise, the Court denied the motion: "It is the Court's conclusion that the state has provided a satisfactory reason for the delay." Wow. In all honesty, the reasoning seemed a major stretch. I was getting an education in the unpredictable ways of the judicial system. No complaints, though. The judge gave us a gift, which maybe was a sign of good things to come. The case would continue. I started looking ahead to trial.

On October 12, 2012, to my shock, Conte filed a motion to allow himself out of prison and be placed on house arrest. In legal jargon, he was asking to be released on his own recognizance. He wanted to live with his mother in Wisconsin until the trial date. Due to some technicality having to do with delay in the proceedings, the Court granted the motion, ordering that Conte wear an electronic monitor. I couldn't believe it. My education continued.

Next up, at the request of the prosecution, the Court ordered a forensic evaluation of Conte. The assigned licensed psychologist found that Conte showed no evidence of mental defect, disease, or impairment, including at the time of the murders. She also found that at the time of the murders Conte had the capacity to form a culpable mental state and appreciate the criminality and consequences of his actions, should he be found guilty, and the capacity to participate in and understand the legal proceedings.

I could have told them all that for free. Evil knows what it wrought.

Trial loomed and I braced.

PART III

17

I HADN'T SEEN, SPOKEN WITH, or heard about Jack Bogard since the special day we were handed our high school diplomas and flung our graduation caps skyward in celebratory anticipation of grand futures. Jack and I had been classmates since seventh grade. He was a good-looking guy, blonde hair, and blue eyes, with a friendly disposition. He generally stayed out of trouble and flew under the high school radar. He ran track, cross-country I believe, but other than that, he led a stay-in-the-shadows high school life, at least that is what I recalled. He didn't hang with the self-styled cool popular kids or the jocks or the druggies, those high school subcultures that drew (or screamed for) attention on campus. And, like most students, Jack pledged allegiance to the mission of the Conway High School All-Star Club—to avoid alcohol and drugs—which, I'm betting, had a realization rate better left unsaid.

I assumed that by now Jack had settled in locally, likely somewhere in Conway or close by, and after finishing his educational journey, found a line of work that suited and sustained him, got married, and was raising a family. Based on early returns by then, he'd be a God-fearing, law-abiding productive member of the community, respectfully going about his daily life with little fanfare. Odd, though, that I hadn't run into him at some local establishment all these years.

So, it was with no small dose of perplexity, and perhaps irony, that days before the criminal trial was set to begin, I learned that Jack Bogard, a name and face from a distant personal past, was slated as a testimonial witness.

How could that possibly be? Jack Bogard will sit in the witness box?

To my memory, Jack's name had not surfaced during the painstakingly thorough criminal investigation in 2002 and 2003. I suppose it was possible that investigators missed something. I had to think that occasionally a glitch happened, even with the best of them.

Had investigators not pursued a lead that first seemed improbable but turned out to be anything but? And what didn't I know about Jack and my father or Jack and Timmy Wayne? If they had a connection, it had eluded me. Or—beyond imagination—did Bogard know Conte? Was he at the murder scene? Or—perish the thought—was he involved?

I was in total darkness and the prosecution wasn't shedding light.

Could this case get any crazier?

In the meantime, we got a new surprise.

The Friday before Monday's start of jury selection, wearing the electronic ankle bracelet, Conte returned to Arkansas from Wisconsin to attend trial. The Court mandated he stay in a hotel under house arrest and the supervision of his attorney. After checking into the hotel, Conte received a visit from a friend, and within minutes, the two nonchalantly bounced from the hotel to make the rounds in Conway. According to Conte's gracious host, "We went to Walmart, got our supplies, water, stuff like that . . . had pizza at Stromboli's, ate at Ruby Tuesday and . . . I think it was Sunday, we played golf."

Played golf? Putting aside how the wheelchair-bound Conte was able to play golf—curious what his handicap was—that he was roaming free literally miles from us on a golf course was beyond outrageous.

His party partner later disclaimed any knowledge that Conte had any movement restrictions: "I had no idea where he can't go and can go. And, you know, cooped up in a hotel room, I figured, 'Hey, Dick, you want to get out and play some golf, you know, and ride around in a golf cart?' So he agreed to that, and we went to the golf course and played nine holes and came home, I think. I don't think we went anywhere after that."

When word of Conte's local globetrotting reached us, I became petrified. First of all, at which golf course did Conte and his chauffeur display their driving and putting skills? The neighborhood where Trey and I lived abutted a golf course. My back yard literally bordered the tenth hole tee. Was Conte hoping to eyeball Trey or me, engage in some classic Conte perverted voyeurism? Was he looking to confront us? Was I being paranoid? In all the years Conte was in our lives, I had never heard one word about him playing golf. And I am guessing he didn't drive and putt from the wheelchair, which gave me "I told you so" bragging rights: the wheelchair was a damn stunt.

The other question was how those monitoring his movements—he hadn't removed that damn electronic bracelet—didn't jump all over this the second the wheelchair hit public ground outside of the hotel and he was, if not footloose, then at least fancy free? I never got an answer.

The good news was that as soon as local law enforcement got word of the escapade, they arrested him for violating the terms of his release and threw his sorry ass back in jail. The judge, who I understood was less than pleased about the shenanigans, revoked his house arrest privileges.

In the end, we were better for it. Conte was back behind bars. But it was another exhausting part of the process. After ten years, I had come to the view that crime victims didn't figure prominently in the goals and values of the criminal justice system. In many ways—in most ways I think—the system existed independent of its victims. Sure, we might play the role of witness in a case or a petitioner at a sentencing hearing or a surrogate for prosecutorial politics. But by and large, crime victims were not essential to the operation of the judicial machinery and, if you wanted to get cynical about it, we sometimes are mere props. The more important players are judges, juries, lawyers, bailiffs, legal staff, law enforcement and investigative personnel, the evidence, other witnesses, and, of course, at center stage here in this shit show, the accused, Dr. Dick Conte. Those of us who lived with the pain of the crime had to make do as best we could, no matter how things played out. I knew in my heart of hearts that eventually I'd have to find a way to let it all go, and then I'd be totally on my own. After the system was done with us, it would bid us good riddance and take up the next case.

But before I could get serious about freeing myself from the system, I had to do the opposite. I had to immerse myself fully in the trial experience. I wanted to be ever-present in the courtroom, breathing in each moment, absorbing everything, from the routine to the dramatic. I wanted to hear every word that spilled from the mouths of witnesses. I wanted to listen intently to the arguments of counsel, even if I didn't grasp the fullness of their advocacy. I wanted to track how the judge, peering down from the elevated bench, handled the trial, see if he betrayed any favoritism or bias, and take a measure of him. I wanted to get a bead on the reactions of jurors as they took in everything they heard and saw, when they nodded, shook their heads, wrote down a note, made a face, or otherwise reacted outwardly to something. I wanted to steal peeks at Conte to see if a beating heart existed inside him and gauge his reactions and divine his thoughts. I wanted to sit in the witness box proudly as a representative of my father, and do whatever I could, however small, to aid the cause.

And, most of all, I wanted to use the trial process to help me move forward and out from under the dark clouds that had eclipsed my soul for so long, aware that at times it would be hurtful to hear certain things.

The night before day one of the trial, after jury selection delivered five men and seven women to the call of civic duty, I felt a strange calm come over me. It had an eeriness to it, like I was about to enter an unfamiliar twilight zone. Maybe it was the calm before the storm. Or maybe instead it was a hint that the pulsating vibes of justice were getting close and preparing to consume the process. I assumed the latter and felt ready.

18

THE MORNING OF JANUARY 15, 2013, I drove to the Faulkner County Courthouse for the start of the trial. I hadn't slept well the night before, and my groggy head spun like a pinwheel while my stomach tossed and turned. I felt some excitement but was mostly paralyzed with fear. I imagined this as the final battle of my life even though it was a battle I wouldn't fight. I was getting a front row seat to watch others clash on my behalf. The thought that the future direction of my family might turn on the outcome of this trial made me nauseous.

My mind tumbled over question after question. Was the prosecution ready? Were they confident or uneasy, or some of both? What drove them? A genuine sense of cause? The pressure to win? The fear of losing?

Were any of the prosecutorial team thinking of our family? Did any awake this morning saying, "today I fight to avenge the Elliotts and Robertsons"? Or did they grab their brief bags after downing their caffeine of choice thinking *Okay, next trial up on the calendar*?

For the defense team, I felt unadulterated hate. In my mind, they were indistinguishable from Conte. How could they defend that horrible human being knowing how guilty he was? How could a human with a soul lay their head on their pillow at night knowing they are defending a murderer, a liar, a kidnapper, and a lunatic? Was it remotely possible they believed in his innocence? And does the suffering of the victims from the crimes their clients commit ever bleed into their consciousness? Or was it all about the money?

Who was going to be in the courtroom besides our family? Would Conte's mother show? Was she, approaching 100, in any condition to travel? Did she have any feelings about us? Had she found empathy—as a mother? Would she acknowledge us? "Sorry for your loss"? What would I say if she did? I wasn't sure I could handle seeing her.

These thoughts escorted me to the parking spot. I wasn't naïve. I knew how the system worked, but I couldn't stem the tide of what I felt.

I eased myself out of the car, met with my brother, and we began to walk in silence across the rear parking lot to the side entry of the courthouse. As we did, I noticed all the cars and media vans. I took a deep breath, reclaimed some calm, and entered the building.

My meditative state expired quickly.

"I don't understand. I can't be in the courtroom? Why not?"

My body stiffened. I was too shocked for anger. It was too nightmarish to be real.

But it was quite real. I was barred from the courtroom.

Without my knowledge, prosecutors and the defense had reached an agreement—what they called a "stipulation"—that I not be allowed to sit in the courtroom during the trial, except when I testified and during closing arguments. Defense lawyers had complained that my courtroom presence might distract the jury and unfairly sway their consideration of the evidence.

Did I do something wrong? Did the prosecution feel I couldn't handle myself?

No, I hadn't done anything wrong. It purportedly had nothing to do with me *per se*. It was a "precaution" to guard against possible "jury bias."

I didn't know what to do with that. The logic escaped me.

As the news settled in, I felt mounting rage. "You've got to be fucking kidding me."

Their explanation went something like this:

"Listen, Ashley, we understand this is upsetting. But please consider the big picture. We feel we have the right guy. We are hopeful of getting a conviction that'll put him away for the rest of his natural life. We want to avoid any possibility that having you in the courtroom gives them an appeal issue. They will do whatever they can to overturn any conviction. We can't hand them anything. We have to keep our eyes on the long game."

I didn't see how my sitting in the courtroom could jeopardize all that. In honesty, of course, I didn't know how those things worked. Still, to my way of thinking, my brother and I and the Robertsons had greater entitlement than anyone to sit in the courtroom during the trial. What happened to public access to courts? Anyone off the street was allowed to take a courtroom seat. And I wasn't just any member of the public. I was the daughter of one of the victims.

I waited ten years-plus for this day, lived and fought for it to happen, prayed for it to happen. Hell, I campaigned for this day to happen. Why wasn't I ensured a front row seat? But in the flash of a cozy lawyerly exchange, without consultation with me, prosecutors flushed my long-awaited moment down the drain. I felt betrayed and disrespected. I felt victimized.

I wondered if Conte had a hand in this. He hated me, apparently. I knew that my parole board performance didn't sit well with him. God forbid that I make a passionate plea to the parole board that he complete his prison term after what he did to my mother and our family. And, knowing me, I probably didn't do a first-rate job of hiding my disapproval of him during his brief and abruptly aborted dalliance with my mother. Yeah, him orchestrating this would be so like the miserable, lowlife asshole he turned out to be.

Anticipating my reaction, and maybe even the unfairness of it all, prosecutors had arranged for Trey and me to sit in a conference room near the courtroom with a baby monitor contraption to listen to the proceedings behind closed doors. That softened the gut punch a little—we weren't being ejected from the building—although it would prove far from the best way to track legal proceedings.

Regardless, I had no choice. I had to accept the "stipulation." I took a deep breath and went to my assigned quarters, head bowed, spirit deflated, and heart pained. It was another reminder that I was collateral damage in this ongoing saga.

My emotional engagement changed a little. Now, something I craved for a decade to experience in all its detail and nuance couldn't be over fast enough. *Let's convict this guy, lick our chops, and be done with it.*

The opening statements were a study in contrast. They were also demoralizing. Maybe I overestimated their importance. Were they mere opening acts, priming the audience for the headliner? Or more significant? Did they naturally hold so much persuasive power a juror might lock into the evidence they were told to expect, but hadn't yet heard? Do jurors make up their minds after opening statements? After listening to these, I sure as hell hoped not.

The prosecution focused on family background, my dad's relationship with Christie, the sequence of events that fateful weekend, the relationship between my mother and Conte, his mercenary tales, and his failed attempt to win my mother back. There were no specifics linking Conte to the murders.

The prosecution said nothing about what they discovered in their searches of Conte's properties. They didn't share results of any forensic analysis. They didn't anticipate Conte alibis relating to Mr. Pringle and the allegedly disabled truck. And, most surprising to me, they didn't project to the jury what likely happened that night, namely, specifically how Conte pulled it off. They pretty much avoided discussion of the actual crimes.

Instead, they delved into the kidnapping detail, as if they were trying that case and not the twin homicides. Was that the game plan?

Try a case another jurisdiction slam-dunked ten years ago and avoid the weaknesses of a case you are supposed to try? The prosecution seemed wary of the holes in their case, as if praying they'd go unnoticed. I didn't get it.

But besides my confusion, I felt doubt, real doubt. Novice that I was, I knew this much: criminal trials were a pitched battle on two sides of a needle being pushed back and forth. The more the needle moved toward doubt, the greater the possibility the defendant walked, and the closer the needle hugged near certainty, the better the chances of a conviction.

I had anticipated that after hearing the prosecution's opening statement, I'd jump for joy, pump my fist in the air, and rejoice that we had this in the bag. It was our opening salvo, our strong foot forward.

I didn't jump for joy. I sagged. I felt swelling doubt.

The defense's opening statement made things worse. They were all-in for doubt.

They tried to evoke sympathy, waxing about Conte's distinguished personal and medical background and how fate dealt him a bad blow with his multiple sclerosis illness and approaching blindness. How could this poor boy in the wheelchair, who dedicated his professional life to saving lives and making the infirm well, do such a ghastly thing? The defense had invoked the power of empathy as a shaper of doubt.

They then launched into a litany of questions that the evidence would leave unanswered, jumping with both feet into the gaping holes the prosecution left in their opening. Where the prosecution didn't venture, the defense plowed with gusto.

They stressed the complete lack of evidence of how the assailant gained entry to the Shady Valley home or how many people were involved. They harped on the lack of an eyewitness, any evidence putting Conte at the scene, or a single neighbor reporting a sound or seeing anything suspicious.

They exalted the crime scene as a treasure trove of doubt—it contained no DNA, fingerprints, saliva, or blood evidence linked to

Conte. They pointed out how the prosecution didn't have a murder weapon or any ballistic evidence that identified a specific weapon or ammo the assailant used that night.

They mentioned the Pringle alibi. They alluded to odometer readings that undercut the prosecution theory about Conte's use of the diesel truck to make the round trip between Arkansas and Utah.

They also attacked the credibility of unidentified "jailhouse witnesses" to a confession. Jailhouse witnesses? A confession? Whoever they were, defense counsel demonized them as "credibility-impaired thieves, burglars, and dopers, one a parole violator, the other a convicted felon that runs around with firearms." Why didn't the prosecution say something about them? Why let Conte's lawyers chop them down before they were even up?

With each point the defense made, I heard in my head, *doubt*! It was doubt after doubt after doubt. It was like a nonstop "cha-ching" each time someone won a prize at an amusement park. I felt I was being treated to a criminal justice riddle: how many doubts did it take to become "reasonable"? I had no idea, but it felt like Conte had moved the needle big time. It felt like he had won the lottery.

Defense counsel ended with a question that flowed naturally from the balance of his opening remarks. He asked the jury, rhetorically, why was the prosecution silent about so many vital factual matters? The answer, he said, was simple: they didn't have direct evidence for any of it. Nothing. All they had was speculation, an obvious euphemism for "reasonable doubt."

I prayed this was round one of many. Because we'd just gotten our butts kicked.

19

WITNESS NUMBER ONE WAS CHRISTIE Vickery, formerly Christie Jameson. After covering her background, the prosecution took her step by step through her movements that weekend, bringing her and the jury to the crime scene discovery.

> **Q:** What did you do upon arrival at Shady Valley?
> **A:** I pulled in the driveway and went to walk in the side garage door. It was locked so I went to the front door.
> **Q:** When you got to the front door, was it locked?
> **A:** No.

The prosecutor then showed Christie and the jury crime scene pictures. I could see that being barred from the courtroom had an upside. I had no interest in looking at the photos.

> **Q:** What happened when you opened that door?
> **A:** The scene that you see in the photos is exactly what I found.
> **Q:** So that picture is accurate as to what you saw when you opened the door?
> **A:** Yes.

Q: How close to the front door was Carter when you opened it?

She didn't answer straight off. I could hear muffled tears. This was hard for her, even after so many years, and I felt bad she had to go through this. I had admittedly been preoccupied with my own pain for ten years. But I wasn't oblivious to the suffering of others outside the family. Christie had endured her own tribulations from this.

I had always liked her, and I resented David Clark, Alan Duke, and Kimberly Duke for prodding investigators to focus on her as a suspect. I wondered if she knew about that. She didn't deserve what they tried to do.

Q: Take your time.
A: I mean, it was hard not to step on him.
Q: Where was Timmy Wayne in relation to Carter?
A: When you walked in the entryway of that home, there was a formal living room over to the left, and he was lying in there.
Q: What did you do at that time?
A: I remember yelling. I remember neighbors in the yard, and I remember they came over or I met them in the yard because I was yelling. I'm sure I asked them to call the police.

That was pretty much it for the prosecution and the defense had nowhere to go with this witness. It was a good start. The crime scene discovery with the photos set the stage.

Next up was Nikki Anderson, a close friend of Christie who was with her that weekend. I didn't at first understand why the prosecution called Nikki, as I suspected her testimony would duplicate Christie's. But when they took a slightly different angle, I saw the wisdom.

Q: How did you enter his home?
A: When we pulled into the driveway we went to the back gate because we thought we were going to a pool party.

Q: What did you find?

A: No one was back there.

Q: How did that strike you?

A: It was really odd because it was a little bit late in the afternoon.

Q: What did you do next?

A: We walked to the front door. It was unlocked.

Q: Was it unusual at Carter's home for the front door to be unlocked?

A: No, not that I remember.

Q: How would you describe his personality?

I did a double take at the question. It came out of nowhere. Why was the prosecution asking this and why ask Nikki, who couldn't know my dad that well? If you wanted to talk about his "personality," I could roll off the tip of my tongue a long list of people much better situated to chronicle Dad's sometimes larger-than-life energy. But why open that can of worms?

A: Honestly, I would just say he's the type of person that everybody liked to be around. He was tons of fun, liked to laugh a lot. A really sweet guy. He was a great businessman so he had tons of friends from business and made friends easily.

Q: I'm going to take you back to that weekend again.

That's it? I didn't get it. The diversion made no sense. I liked what she said but feared defense counsel would have a field day with her now. She had also crossed over from "personality" to his skills as a businessman. I feared the defense would plumb the depths of the wrongheaded theories that initially surfaced about my father, the drug dealing, the gambling, the mob hit, the jealous husband, and business deals gone south. Did the prosecution unwittingly invite the defense to put on an evidentiary sideshow?

Q: What did you find when you opened the front door?"

A: Well, Christie opened the door first and she was angry because he hadn't been taking her phone calls the whole way back from Memphis, and I could kind of see that he was on the ground in front of the door but I couldn't see much because she walked in first and just turned around, didn't say a word. The look on her face, I knew something was terribly wrong but I assumed he had probably had a heart attack. And so she ran out. I couldn't get very far in the front door because Carter was on the ground and there was another person who I didn't know in the formal living room to my left. I turned around and ran with her to the neighbor's yard.

She seemed to by holding back tears. It was hard for her, too. I wish I could see how the jury was reacting.

Q: Take your time. Did anything catch your attention besides the obvious when you walked in and saw that foyer?

A: Two things struck me as extremely odd. Carter seemed to be on the ground as if he hadn't fallen. His hands were by his side. That was odd because he was extremely athletic and energetic, and just his personality, he never would have let somebody put a gun to his head and then lie down on the ground. The other thing that struck me as odd is that nothing seemed disturbed in the immediate area, including a tall table with glass bowls and candles that, every time I went to his house I thought "I need to stay away from that table." It was sitting there, in perfect order.

Q: And it looked like it always did, is that fair to say?

A: Looked like it always had.

And that was it for Nikki. Despite invitations to go far afield, the defense had nothing in response. Nikki had given the jury a more in-depth feel for the crime scene, stoking curiosity about how it happened.

It was clear her testimony was rehearsed, but that I assume is normally the case, as it would be for me as well. Two witnesses in, and the prosecution had tugged at juror heartstrings with photos, and had laid some foundation for a well-prepared murder by someone who knew something about killing.

I could see the glimmers of a slow reconstruction of what happened, and became curious about how the prosecution planned to build the rest without direct evidence. I'd have to wait to learn, because the next person to take the oath was my mother. I was nervous for her.

Prosecutors started with the usual background, how Mom met Conte, when they started dating, what they did on dates, and getting engaged and then married with two ceremonies, civil and church. Then prosecutors made an interesting play. They showed my mother pictures of Conte from when they were together, and asked two revealing questions.

> **Q:** Now, I don't mean to state the obvious or sound insensitive, but the defendant is here today in a wheelchair. It appears in those pictures that he was not in a wheelchair. Is that accurate?
> **A:** That's *very* accurate.

I could tell that her mild but noticeable emphasis on "very" was not spontaneous.

> **Q:** How would you describe his overall health and fitness at the time?
> **A:** He was very robust, fit, and athletic. He did long hikes with heavy packs on his back to stay in shape. He was very robust.

Three "verys" in two answers—not bad, Mom.

It was a short but effective counterpoint to the image of Conte in a wheelchair. In a matter of seconds, the prosecution reminded the jury that the person on trial was not the pathetic-looking and beaten down man before them in his dramatic wheelchair prop. It was the "fit and robust" person in the photos, beating a manly path in the wilderness with faux military regalia.

It also was an effective prelude to what came next.

Q: Were there some intriguing things that he told you about his past?

A: Yes.

Q: Please tell the jury about that?

A: He told me that when he was in high school, he was a championship wrestler and was recruited by a company called the Vinnell Corporation, a military undercover operation. He said the U.S. government employed him as a mercenary, as a hired killer.

The defense interrupted and objected. The prosecutors had drawn blood. In a flash, "Wheelchair Conte" had been effectively transformed into "Killer Conte," and the defense wanted to stop the hemorrhaging.

Defense counsel argued that all the talk about traveling to dark, dangerous places abroad, killing the enemy, and working with the CIA, was a sideshow or, in legal jargon, not relevant. The prosecution pushed back, pointing out that traveling to kill is precisely what the case was about. Whether the stuff of fantasy or not, the prosecutor urged, my mom's testimony gave the jury insight into Conte's self-portrayal, the person, down deep, he fancied himself.

The Court responded: "I have to admit, it's interesting he made these statements about a life he made up. But if he wasn't any of those things, the relevance may be tenuous. But I'm going to overrule the objection. I'm going to let him go ahead and make the inquiry."

We dodged a bullet. It had to be a major blow to the defense. The jury was granted admission to the Conte fantasy world. The prosecution piled on.

Q: During the time that he was telling you these stories, did he have an alias that he went by?

A: He did. His alias was "Paladin." And he called the place where he lived in Carson City "Paladin Arms." He had a trademark too, a stamp he would put on top of his stationery and business card, "Have gun, will travel."

"Paladin" was a fictional character in the TV show *Have Gun —Will Travel* that aired on CBS in the late 1950s and early '60s. Paladin was an investigator and gunfighter who traveled the Old West as a gun for hire. When on the clock, he donned all-black Western-style clothing, and while he had an avowed preference to fix client problems diplomatically, his non-violent solutions were more exception than rule. Conte was a Paladin wannabe.

Q: Do you recall specific stories he told you?

A: Yes. I remember one where he had gone to Cambodia for a special mission as a special operations person. He knew I loved white roses. He wrote that while in his military combat gear, he avoided the guards walking back and forth in front of the Cambodian Emperor's rose garden, and managed to get inside where he stole a rose for me. They didn't have white, so he grabbed a yellow rose and pressed it into a book to bring to me.

I hadn't heard this story before. It was drenched in insanity. I knew Conte was a nut job. But the Cambodia story was over the top, an imaginative corroboration of an unstable mind.

The prosecution was on a roll. They had my mother talk about the dog tags Conte wore; wings the military gave him for passing training in parachuting; how his cabin, with all its military paraphernalia, served as a military safe house for his friends, also in "Special Ops," to recuperate; the vast weaponry he possessed, including knives in each of his jacket pockets; the surveillance cameras and bugging devices in his cabin; and mercenary magazines and war movie videos. It was quite the visual.

Prosecutors had recast Conte entirely from what his attorneys tried to construct in the opening statement. Then they moved deeper into the heart.

Q: How did your relationship go at that point?

A: It began to deteriorate after I saw these things in the house. I mean, I loved him and we had married. I wanted to make it work.

I could hear soft tears through the baby monitor. My mother could call up her Scarlett O'Hara with the best of them. Maybe they were genuine tears. I didn't care, so long as the jury thought so. In fairness, she did try to make it work. But I never thought she loved him. She thought he could give her the lifestyle she craved. And when she saw he was worse than bargain basement, she booked on him.

Q: You're getting emotional. Some of those things we're gonna talk about in a minute.

A: Okay, okay.

Q: How did it go when you told Dick it wasn't working out, that you could not live that way? Can you talk to the jury about that?

A: It didn't go well at all. I told him I was very unhappy and it wasn't going to work out. I wanted a divorce.

Q: How did he react?

A: He was very upset. He started to cry. He began to beg me not to divorce him. It would humiliate and embarrass him. He was incredibly upset.

Q: Did he tried to win you back?

A: Yes.

Q: How specifically?

A: He sent me flowers, often at work, as well as romantic cards sprayed with perfume. I have a hundred cards. He sometimes would sneak into my condo and place the cards in a book, in lingerie drawers, and sometimes on the refrigerator. He also bought me gifts, including jewelry.

Q: So he had access to your condo in Salt Lake City?

A: Yes, I had a combination lock on my front door, which he knew.

The defense objected again. They anticipated what was coming, and it was the number one Conte make-believe highlight. The attorneys and the judge went back and forth on its relevance. But at this point, it seemed the judge had let all the cats out of the bag. How could he now stop the parade? These stories filled out the criminal mind of Conte. They went to motive, why he did what he did. Latching onto "state of mind," the Court overruled the objection.

Q: On or about April the 17, 2002, did you receive a disturbing phone call from the defendant?

A: I did.

Q: Please tell the jury about that phone call

A: When I picked up the phone, as I said hello, I could hear gunfire, like machine guns going off in the background, like it was a war zone. It was Dick. He said "Lark."

Q: What did you say?

A: I said, "Dick, what's going on? Where are you?"

Q: What did he say?

A: He said, "I'm in Afghanistan. I'm pinned under a truck and they're gonna kill me any moment. I wanted to call and tell you that I love you. This might be the last time we ever talk to each other."

Q: How did you react?

A: I was like, "Oh, my God," you know, and I said, "Be careful."

Q: What happened next?

A: We were disconnected.

Q: When was the next time you saw him?

A: I next saw him in Salt Lake in the first part of May. He came to show me where he had been shot in Afghanistan.

The prosecution let that hang for a bit and then changed subjects. They briefly explored how my mother and Conte stayed in touch notwithstanding the pending divorce, how she knew his work schedule, and that he wasn't working the weekend of May 17, 2002. They then focused on the murders.

Q: Did you also talk to Conte about the circumstances around the murders of Carter Elliott and Timmy Wayne?

A: Yes.

Q: Did the defendant ever make any statements to you about the crime scene?

A: Yes, he did.

Q: What did he say?

A: He told me that when a bullet is left next to the victim, it is the signature of the killer, and that you should be quiet about it. He called it a "spent bullet."

Based on the opening statement, the prosecution had one more major play and I wondered whether the Court would allow it, even though the judge had tacitly approved during opening statements. It struck me as prejudicial but, again, what did I know?

Q: I'd like to take you to June 20, 2002.

A: Okay.

Q: Did you go to work that day?

A: I did.

Q: Did you come home from work?

A: I did.

Q: Please tell the jury what happened when you arrived home on that Thursday evening.

Defense counsel shot up, objecting. They could ill afford to have the jury hear the kidnapping details. We had arrived at a pivotal part of the case.

The judge preempted the lawyer tussle: "Well, we're not trying him on kidnapping. Let's not go through a blow-by-blow, step-by-step. If you want to ask her a couple of general questions, you may."

It seemed a win for the defense. "A couple of general questions." How much damage could prosecutors inflict with that limitation? What followed left my head shaking.

Q: When you came home, was the defendant there?
A: Yes. He was.
Q: Was armed with anything?
A: He had a stun gun.
Q: During the time he was in your home, did he tie you down?
A: He did.

A "couple of general questions" but no "blow-by-blow"? I couldn't believe the defense wasn't jumping up and down and frothing at the mouth. The prosecution, with no hint of subtlety, was running roughshod over the judge's ruling and the defense was acquiescing. Why stop now?

Q: Did he force you to drink something?
A: He did.
Q: Did he threaten to kill you?
A: He did.
Q: Did he do anything else to you?
A: Yes.

Q: What?

A: I woke up handcuffed in the back of his pickup truck.

Q: Now, during this time period, did he express his hurt feelings over what you had done to him?

A: Yes. He did. He was crying and threatening to kill himself, threatening to kill me. He was distraught.

Q: Tell the jury, please, about what happened in the truck.

A: I was passed out and would wake up off and on, until we got to Carson City, Nevada.

Q: What happened when you got to Nevada?

A: I woke up and he handcuffed me to the posts of his Paul Bunyan bed.

I liked the Paul Bunyan touch. Wilderness boy dominating his woman. Nice image.

Q: Did you eventually get free?

A: Yes. A friend got me out of there and I eventually went to the hospital.

A "couple of general questions" became, without a hiccup, a long-detailed Q&A that portrayed Conte as a felonious madman. True, they didn't get into the evidence of what happened in the Salt Lake condo and the graves Conte dug on his property in contemplation of a planned murder-suicide. Nor did they tell the jury about his long imprisonment. But they inflicted serious damage.

Finally, my mother confirmed a small but important detail. Investigators found pictures of my family, including my father, in Conte's cabin. Conte had never met my father and didn't know what he looked like. My mother never gave Conte the photos. He had no reason to have them. The implication was clear: Conte stole the photos from the Salt Lake condo so he could recognize my father when he landed at Shady Valley on May 18.

Defense counsel took over. He got my mother to confirm a few things—that Conte held a federal firearms license and was an authorized dealer and importer of firearms and his Paladin business card supported those pursuits. He also got Mom to acknowledge she never told Conte she wanted anything bad to happen to my father. They never discussed the subject. She admitted, too, that they both left the Nevada cabin on June 20 of their own accord, before police arrived.

The defense closed with the following examination.

Q: Were you interviewed by Sergeant Barrett, now Lieutenant Barrett, of the Conway Police Department a couple of weeks after Mr. Elliott's death?

A: Yes.

Q: You never told Sgt. Barrett about the alleged conversation you testified about today, that Dr. Conte said something about a bullet left at the scene of the crime being a signature, did you?

A: I don't think so.

Q: And up until that day at your apartment, including during the many months you allowed him to help pay for your condo, you never were fearful of him. Is that a fair statement?

A: That's a fair statement.

Q: In fact, during the entire time from when you announced the end of the marriage to Dr. Conte, three months after you took the marital vows in a church, until the death of Mr. Elliott, Dr. Conte was nothing but kind to you and your children, correct?

A: That's fair.

Q: Yes, fair. And you continued to accept during that time all his romantic offerings as he attempted to win you back, correct?

A: Uh, I guess.

Q: You guess? You never protested that he stop, did you?

A: No, I guess not.

Q: It is also true, is it not, that when Mr. Elliott was killed, you never once mentioned to the investigators you thought the killer was Dr. Conte, correct?

A: Yes, that is true.

Q: In fact, you suggested to them that it was a professional hit and likely had to do with money, correct?

A: That is what I thought at the time.

Q: And that's what you told them, right?

A: I think so.

Q: Well, let's be specific. You specifically told investigators that your ex-husband likely quote "got in over his head" closed quote and that somebody hired someone to kill him because quote "he didn't pay them" closed quote or quote "he knew something he shouldn't know" closed quote, correct?

A: I believe that's what I said at the time.

The defense ended its direct examination on that note. I wanted so much to see how that line of questioning landed with the jury. It had definitely landed with me. Credit the defense, especially the point about my mother's initial theory. She would know better than anyone and, while she is not an investigator and in truth gave a seat-of-the-pants opinion, the testimony easily could have made inroads with the jury.

Prosecutors had one more shot. They wanted to introduce a photo. It seemed simple enough. It was not. The defense objected.

The photo depicted Conte's silver diesel truck connected by a tow bar to his red Jeep. It showed that the diesel truck was roughly twice the size of the Jeep. The picture had writing on the back, supposedly in Conte's hand. They went back and forth until the Court resolved to admit the photo without the handwriting. My mother confirmed that Conte owned both vehicles in May 2002. I didn't understand the hoopla. I would later.

My mother had been a star. She delivered everything the prosecution wanted in concise terms and a convincing tone. I was proud of her. But I was learning, step by step, that in this trial, at least, counting unhatched chickens is unwise: you never know what's coming next and how it might turn the tables.

20

KEVIN CLARK, MY UNCLE BY marriage to my mom's sister, took the stand next. I wondered how he'd show up. Would he cling to residual allegiance to his longstanding pal, fellow physician, and hunting partner? Would he feel conflicted or put distance between them? Would he display remorse for introducing Conte into our lives? Would it matter to him that Conte did some bad things to the sister of his wife? Where did those events leave him emotionally? I didn't know, although I was reminded that Clark never visited Conte during the Nevada incarceration, a no-show that didn't sit well with Conte.

Clark affirmed that he and Conte were "close friends." It was an inevitable admission that helped the cause. Testimony from a former close friend should enjoy implied credibility. Then, the prosecution dove right in.

Conte loved firearms and was adept at using them. He told Clark he "was a contract killer for the Vinnell Corporation and for the U.S. government" and sometimes provided evidence of his mercenary "missions," for example, displaying medals that confirmed he was part of "the Delta Force Mission into Iran in 1979."

Then the following astonishing exchange took place.

Q: On April 17, 2002, did you get a disturbing phone call from Dick Conte?

A: Yes.

Q: Tell the jury what happened during that phone call.

A: He said he'd been in Afghanistan trapped under an SUV and had been sniped at and had several bullets in him they wouldn't let him take out in Afghanistan. He wanted me to take them out. He was being flown back to Dugway, Utah where he would meet me at my office a few hours later.

Q: Did he show up?

A: Yes.

Q: How did he appear when he showed up at your office?

A: He was in full battle fatigues, boots, Kevlar vest and helmet. He undid his vest and bullets fell out from the breastplate onto the floor of my office.

A: After you saw his condition, what did you do?

Q: I took him to the hospital and took X-rays and then took him back to my office and removed the bullets that were under the skin outside of his Kevlar vest.

Q: Can you tell the jury what you saw?

A: There were, as I recall, eight or nine bullets from his legs, arm, and shoulder.

Q: Did they appear consistent with gunshot wounds?

A: No.

Q: How did they appear to you?

A: They looked like they had been inserted through small incisions.

Q: Did it appear to you based on your medical experience and training, that he had been shot?

A: No.

The prosecution moved on. But I didn't. I was trapped inside that testimony. Did my Uncle Kevin confront Conte about his transparent trickery? Based on the testimony, it seemed not. And shouldn't he have sounded an alarm, at least to my mother and me, that this guy was so off the wall to be dangerous? I mean, that little episode wasn't a teenage prank that warranted a mild headshake and a "boys will be boys" comment. Wasn't it clear then, if it had not been earlier, that Conte was horribly unstable and possibly mad and capable of heinous things? Did he tell my mom and she didn't tell me?

Maybe the answers weren't relevant to the criminal case, but they seemed important to understanding how someone married to my aunt chose to handle serious risks facing the family. Conte was using Clark, his "close friend," to play a cameo role in his own continued fantasy. He got Clark to do him a solid and Clark, based on the testimony at least, seemed to play along.

Clark also testified about a letter he and my Aunt Gaye got from Conte during the kidnapping. After some fighting among the attorneys, the Court let him read the letter to the jury:

"Lark picked up some guy on the internet and went to his house and killed him. She is convinced she will go to prison, called me at the cabin. She locked herself out of the guy's house so I couldn't clean up and she didn't want me to break in, left her DNA all over his fucking penis. I gave her my ten-thousand-dollar doomsday cash and I'm taking her to Vegas. She'll buy a car with new plates and papers and drive to the gulf coast. I'll try to set her up in a company safe house. I think it's up over my head. I have to work tomorrow. Of course she hasn't had sex with me since the end of February but will do it with a stranger. She is totally flipped out about not going to prison and not getting old and wrinkled. I will go back to Salt Lake City as soon as I can and will keep an eye on the news to see what develops. I cannot believe this. If I had been a good enough husband, she would be okay. I've got to run back. She is packing everything."

The letter reaffirmed the imprint of a sick and devious individual who had blurred the distinctions in his psyche between narcissistic fantasies and reality. You had to wonder whether Conte had completely lost the ability to tell the difference, that whatever moral code he had at one time was now reduced to shambles and replaced with an amalgam of self-justifications.

As prosecutors wrapped up the Clark testimony, I was summoned to testify. The time had come for me to stand for my father and do what I could, however small, to avenge him. I knew I didn't have a lot to offer. But I had to do what I could.

Entering the courtroom, I began to channel a powerful flow of merged emotions. I had to focus, so I fixated on the only thing I could: Conte. He looked pitiful his phony wheelchair. My legs wobbled as I walked past him to the witness box. I said "I do" to the testimonial oath in a voice I didn't recognize. I told the judge I needed a minute to get composed. He accommodated me. I asked for a tissue. I gathered myself. The questions began. They were easy volleys to start, about my background, relationship with my father, familiarity with Timmy Wayne, how I met Conte, and my attendance at the church wedding of him and Mom.

Then the prosecution asked me to identify Conte in the courtroom. I stared right at him and pointed with the evilest eye I could. My eyes filled with tears. I felt pure hatred for him in that moment, a consuming feeling that rattled my heart. I began to tremble. I want to go at him, pummel him with punches. I wanted to push him over in his ridiculous wheelchair and watch him get up, to shock everyone.

I tried to stop the onslaught of my rage. I couldn't. I started to cry. I tried to stop crying. I couldn't, and then I didn't want to stop. I didn't care where I was. I wanted the pain in my tears to rob the air around Conte and suffocate the bastard. Let him drop dead and end this nightmare.

I was approaching hysterical. The lawyers approached the bench. Conte's lawyer complained that I kept staring at Conte. The prosecutor referred to me as "a pretty emotional person." To both charges, I plead guilty. The judge halted the proceedings. Someone gave me water. I took a gulp. It helped. The judge called a recess. I was escorted out of the courtroom.

Holy shit. What a testimonial debut.

I met briefly with the prosecution. I knew I had to keep my shit together. I called on the spirit of my heavenly father to give me the strength and composure to represent my earthly father well. I calmed down. I nodded to the prosecutors to signal I was ready. They nodded back. We returned to the courtroom. Fifteen minutes after my display of emotion, we resumed. I was drained but ready.

The questions focused on my relationship with Conte during the time he was with my mother, his buying me my wedding dress, how I learned about the murder of my father, Dad's funeral, and my finding the gun at my father's house that we turned over to the police. But most questions focused on the kidnapping, again without defense objection. After discussing that night's early events, we arrived at my telephone call with Conte as he held my mother captive.

Q: When you eventually spoke to Dick, tell the jury what happened.

A: I remember that Dick told me if I ever needed anything concerning my mother to please contact him because he would help me, and so I began to try to find him and talk to him. And when I called him, I was extremely upset at him. I said, "Where's my mother?" He said, "What do you mean?" I said, "Where's my mother?" And he said, "Oh, calm down. Don't call the police."

Q: How did you respond?

A: I said, "It's too late. I've already called them."

Q: Did he respond?

A: Yes, he said, "No, no, no, no, no. Your mom picked up a man in Park City and she slept with him and she killed him and I've given her money and I've taken her down to the border in Mexico and you're never going to see her again."

I started to cry again. The prosecutor told me to "take a second." I needed more than one. But I dug in deep and regained my composure. The prosecutor continued.

Q: Did that sound like your mom?

A: No, it didn't sound like my mom at all.

Q: Did you confront him with that?

A: Yes.

Q: How did he respond?

A: I don't remember how he responded. I started screaming at him and hung up.

After a couple of more questions, the prosecution "passed the witness"—such a charming phrase, as if we are inanimate objects lawyers toss around like footballs.

The defense wanted to ask me about my political support for Cody Hiland and how I lobbied for a prosecutor who'd bring charges. They argued it would show my witness bias. Well, duh. Of course I was biased. Was that a news flash to the defense, that a daughter might be biased against the person she felt killed her father? I'd be the first to admit it. In all events, the Court disallowed the questions. Notch one for the rational mind.

And that was about it. The defense asked about missing money and diamonds, but I had no first-hand knowledge. The prosecution had no redirect, which I guess is a witness badge of honor after a cross-examination.

I returned to my assigned cave, amped up. I knew I hadn't contributed much, other than the force of my emotion. But I felt I'd helped the cause a little, if only a single nail in Conte's coffin. Most of all, I hoped my dad, wherever his spirit, knew I had his back.

The next two witnesses were my brother, Trey, and our Uncle Richard Gathright. No reflection on either, but neither appearance moved the needle one way or the other. The most significant part of what my brother said was describing his phone call with Conte during the kidnapping when Conte threatened to kill himself and broke into tears. That pretty much echoed the testimony of my mother and me. Gathright had a similar call with Conte during the kidnapping ordeal.

More interesting—to no one probably but me—was the Court allowed Trey to stay in the courtroom when his testimony concluded. Not me, however. I had to stay in the conference room. While I appreciated the judge didn't want another outburst from me, I also felt I had an absolute right to remain. So what if I lost it on the stand? I was confident it wasn't the first time a victim let loose some tears in a criminal trial. I had rallied and knew I could hold it together now that I was a mere spectator. They never gave me the chance and, as far as I was concerned, that was flat-out wrong.

In either event, the last family members to testify opened the way for the investigative phase of the prosecution's case. I became unsteady anticipating what was coming. While the investigation by all indications was thorough and professional—I continued to be impressed by the diligence and dedication that law enforcement showed—when it came to the nitty-gritty, direct evidence was wanting. The prosecutorial case so far as I could tell was, of necessity, a stitched patchwork of circumstantial evidence, apart from the kidnapping evidence. The wide and fragile seams in the quilt kept me continuously on edge.

They began with Rick Brown, a Nevada investigator with the Douglas County Sheriff's Office (DCSO) who headed up a search of the Conte Nevada cabin.

Brown's people discovered a book titled *The Quiet Killer*, a tome that instructs on the use of suppressors and how to execute people quietly. They also found several documents loosely connecting Conte to the scene of crime, including two on which Conte scribbled "Edmond Carter Elliott, Conway, Arkansas" and "No. 6 Shady Valley Road" and "Detco," my father's company, as well as Detco's phone number. In addition, they found computer printouts of online searches for police, federal and emergency radio frequencies for the Conway area, and an internet street map of Conway, all dated May 11, 2002, a week before.

These materials connected Conte to Conway, a place he swore he'd never visited. Why else would Conte have them unless he was planning something untoward there? For sure, he wasn't throwing a surprise party. How would defense counsel deal with this evidence, other than ignore it? It seemed damning to me.

The prosecution, surprisingly, didn't ask any questions of Brown about William Pringle, the deceased alibi witness who Brown interviewed. Didn't it make sense to steal some of the defense thunder there? An alibi witness was dangerous. If believed, that testimony alone could give Conte the keys to freedom. If Pringle were to spring from the grave and appear in this trial, it would only be in the person of Investigator Brown. Why not anticipate this?

So, when the defense cross-examined Brown regarding Pringle, it wrote on a clean slate, and inflicted damage.

> **Q:** Did Mr. Pringle tell you he saw Dr. Conte at Duck Creek over the weekend at issue, in May of 2002?
>
> **A:** Yes, sir.
>
> **Q:** Did he tell you Dr. Conte had his truck towed from the cabin on or about May 20?
>
> **A:** Yes, sir.
>
> **Q:** And did he tell you he had seen Dr. Conte driving his truck the day before?
>
> **A:** I believe he said he saw Dr. Conte drive his truck during that weekend three or four times.

Three or four times. I wondered whether defense counsel glanced at the jury.

The defense also got Brown to admit that investigators didn't interview anyone else in the immediate area of Duck Creek, Utah who could have seen Conte that weekend. That confused me. Didn't they want to corroborate the Pringle statements if possible? Far be it for me to want to help the Conte cause, but I wondered what the jury felt about the failure to interview others.

The prosecution came back by getting Brown to testify Pringle told him Conte had to "remind" him about seeing Conte that weekend. In other words, Pringle's memory or, worse, veracity, was thrown into question. Pringle also told Brown that Conte acted "strange" and didn't look him "in the eye" when they discussed Conte's whereabouts.

Unless the jury thought Pringle was lying—and I heard nothing to suggest that—or he simply recalled incorrectly—more possible for sure—the defense had planted fertile seeds of doubt in the case.

The defense wasn't done with Brown. He authenticated two receipts showing Conte purchased 53 gallons of diesel fuel on May 16 and 49 gallons on May 22. Defense counsel didn't probe further, and on re-direct, the prosecution ignored the evidence. I assumed we'd hear more about this evidence later. The issue whether Conte could have managed the round-trip journey that weekend continued to hover in the air. It was as if both sides were tiptoeing around the issue. I had to think a reckoning lay ahead.

The prosecution next called Charles McLemore, formerly an investigator with the Arkansas State Police. McLemore participated in the joint search of the Conte cabin in Carson City, with the Conway PD, the FBI, and DCSO.

McLemore first told the jury about a book found at the cabin, titled *The History of Torture and Execution*. It was another emblem of Conte's dark soul. The more shit like this they pulled from his place, the more likely it became clear Conte operated within the swamp of criminal behavior.

McLemore also provided the strongest evidence so far that tied Conte to the crime.

> **Q:** When you conduced a search of Conte's cabin in Carson City, were you looking for anything in particular?
>
> **A:** Yes, we were looking for pistols that shot 9mm shells. We were looking for Glaser Safety Slugs. We were looking for .45s or .45 Glaser Safety Slugs, barrels, clips or magazine, anything that would correspond with the criminal case evidence we had.
>
> **Q:** During that search, did you personally locate several firearms in the residence?
>
> **A:** Yes.

Q: What does that response mean?

A: Anywhere you wanted one. I mean, they were everywhere.

Q: Okay.

A: And loaded.

The photos showed that Conte literally maintained a weapons arsenal in his cabin. According to one investigator, a firearm literally was within reach no matter where you stood in the place. They had never seen anything like it.

Q: Mr. McLemore, during the search and seizure at that residence, did you seize an H&K firearm?

A: Yes, sir.

Q: Did you also locate a magazine that went with that firearm?

A: Yes, sir.

Q: What caliber of ammunition does it shoot?

A: Nine-millimeter (9mm).

Q: Looking at exhibit 98, what type of ammunition is that?

A: It's called Glaser Safety Slug. It has a blue tip.

Q: How many bullets does the magazine hold?

A: Fifteen.

Q: How many did you find?

A: Fourteen.

Q: Can the firearm hold more?

A: Yes, it could have one in the chamber.

Q: For a total of sixteen?

A: Yes.

Q: If two bullets were used to kill two people, one each, out of this firearm fully loaded, fourteen would remain?

A: Yes, sir.

Q: And that is what you found?

A: Yes, sir.

Q: Now, Mr. McLemore, during your search of the residence, did you also locate a Star 9mm firearm?

A: Yes, sir.

Q: And how many bullets can that firearm hold?

A: Seven.

Q: How many did you find?

A: Six.

Q: So, if the perpetrator brought the 9mm firearm to the scene, and discharged a chamber round with a fully loaded magazine, six would remain in the clip, correct?

A: Yes.

I thought, wow. The math worked out perfectly. Three rounds were used at the scene, two to kill and one unfired and dislodged from the chamber. Three rounds were missing from the magazines in identical types of firearms at the cabin. Could the defense possibly categorize the matching of the numbers as coincidence? I couldn't imagine.

The only issue, I assumed, was whether ballistics could align the used rounds and the seized gun barrels. Based on opening statements, the answer seemed negative. The next round of questions shed light.

Q: Mr. McLemore, let me ask you, can you change barrels out on firearms?

A: Yes, sir.

Q: So, changing the barrel of a discharged firearm would make it difficult to conduct an effective ballistics test, correct?

A: Yes, absolutely.

The implication was plain. Conte may have changed barrels to foil ballistics. But how and when? We probably would never know. He could have tossed the barrels into the Arkansas River en route to Utah. He knew how to make sure the barrels took up permanent residence at the river bottom—recall he instructed me on how to do the same with a dead body—and easily could have found a safe spot along the way to make it happen. The case was taking shape.

21

THE MCLEMORE TESTIMONY STRUCK ME as the closest to direct evidence that investigators had assembled. To my non-lawyer mind, the local map and radio frequencies were compelling evidence of premeditation, a Conte plan to descend, undetected, upon Conway, by creeping under law enforcement radar. And, putting aside the gun barrel evidence, the fact that investigators found in his cabin the same kind of weapons used in the crimes—with their magazines missing bullets that lined up with what was found at the scene—came damn close to closing another loop.

I was beginning to see how this worked, these individual pieces of a puzzle, put in place painstakingly through each witness, until little was left to the imagination. The ultimate question, of course, was whether the prosecution could assemble enough pieces to complete the picture, or enough of it at least to ward off reasonable doubt. They were on their way, and I was impressed. But we had a ways to go.

The next witness was Lt. Jim Barrett, the lead investigator. Lt Barrett had always struck me as thoroughly professional, super smart, and straightforward, and I held him in high regard. He treated my family with respect and was consistently supportive. I was confident that he'd lend credibility to the investigation and fill in remaining blanks.

He spent considerable time on the stand. The prosecution first established his impressive *bona fides* as an investigator and then they got to it. Here is what struck me as most important.

> Q: Lieutenant, did anything you found in the house help you exclude a home invasion?
>
> A: Yes, we found several things that were extremely inconsistent with a home invasion robbery.
>
> Q: Please explain.
>
> A: I saw an expensive looking Rolex watch.
>
> Q: Anything else?
>
> A: Yes, we found televisions and other electronics, large visible sums of cash, and a visible firearm.
>
> Q: How much cash?
>
> A: Over sixteen thousand dollars.
>
> Q: What did that discovery say to you?
>
> A: All, in my experience, would have been prime targets for a home invasion robbery, that an invader would definitely take prior to exiting.
>
> Q: Did you see signs of forced entry?
>
> A: No, I did not.

This was a preemptive strike that undermined any defense theory of a robbery and thus limited opportunities for Conte's attorneys to corrupt the minds of jurors with confusion. Lt. Barrett deftly closed that door.

The prosecution then walked Lt. Barrett through the crime scene photos in painstaking detail. It was another moment when I was pleased to be outside the courtroom. While I so wanted to see juror reactions to what was shown. I was equally happy not to see what they saw.

> Q: Lieutenant Barrett, what is that laying on top of Mr. Elliott?
>
> A: A folded white cotton towel we found on the back of his head.

Q: Did you notice anything out of the ordinary?

A: It had two holes through the various layers of the folded fabric consistent with being made by a firearm.

Q: What was its significance?

A: It appeared that the perpetrator, in addition to maybe using a suppressor or silencer, had used towels to muffle the sound and limit the splatter of blood.

This evidence resonated with the perceived Conte game plan—to quietly kill without leaving a trace. It explained why neighbors, literally a stone's throw away, heard nothing.

But Conte made a mistake that Lt. Barrett figured out.

Q: Earlier you talked about a cap belonging to Timmy Wayne.

A: Yes, sir.

Q: What did you find in the cap?

A: We found an unfired .45 ACP, automatic Colt pistol cartridge, which we determined was a blue tip Glaser Safety Slug.

Q: Had you ever seen one before?

A: Never in the commission of a crime, only in gun shops, usually kept behind the counter in six-round packages. It's extremely expensive.

An unfired round had been left at the scene. Recall that my mother testified that Conte told her that a left round was an executioner signature. I will admit, it was a rather good explanation. But Lt. Barrett had a different theory. Like we often see in film, when someone holding a firearm wants somebody's attention, he racks the slide of the firearm to make a noise to convey he means business. That's what happened here, Barrett's theory went. Conte jacked a round out of the chamber to the floor to make a point to his captives, and the round came to rest inside Timmy Wayne's cap. And although Conte policed the brass he used to kill, the unfired round wasn't easily found in the darkness of the foyer, and, not seeing it right away, and knowing he couldn't dawdle, Conte left it at the scene. That round helped investigators match used rounds at the scene with missing rounds in the magazines found in the Conte cabin.

Lt. Barrett also helped with the time of the crime. The earlier in the night that the killings were made, the more likely Conte had time to get back to Utah on Sunday May 19 for the landline call he made around 10 p.m. Mountain time. Too much later, after midnight or into the morning, as the defense urged, Conte would probably not have had enough time to kill and still access the landline at that time.

Q: Did you receive any evidence that informed the time of the crime?
A: Yes. We found a Taco Bell receipt, which had been retrieved from the trash can in the kitchen.
Q: I am showing the exhibit. What does the time stamp state?
A: May 18, 2002 at 8:51 and twelve seconds in the evening.

The receipt alone didn't do the trick. We needed autopsy evidence. But it provided a starting point for the argument.

There was also the question of the vehicles. Investigators presumed he used the diesel truck. Barrett had a hunch that dead bugs entangled in the front grate or the engine might be informative. Could bug remnants be indigenous to a region and, if so, what did they show here? He sent an insect sample to a forensic entomologist. But the results yielded nothing of value. Apparently, we all have the same bugs. The mystery of the vehicles remained.

On a related issue, Barrett scored with phone records. His sleuthing determined that Conte didn't make any landline calls from late in the evening on May 16 through the late evening of May 19. That meant, to the extent Conte made any calls—and Conte was a chatterbox—he used his cell phone, implying he was away from his residence for the entire weekend.

On cross-examination, the defense tried to poke holes in the prosecution time of death. They focused on the Taco Bell time stamp of 8:51 p.m.

> **Q:** Did you determine whether or not that time stamp was accurate on that receipt?
>
> **A:** Based on the information I received, yes, it appeared to be accurate.
>
> **Q:** Did you run a receipt through the register to compare it against your watch for a time?
>
> **A:** No, sir, I didn't.

The defense also tried to resurrect the robbery theory.

> **Q:** Did you have information there was more cash than what was found in the house?
>
> **A:** I had been told that at one point in time, yes, sir.
>
> **Q:** And did you ever locate a larger amount of cash that belonged to Mr. Elliott other than what was in the house?
>
> **A:** The only cash that I found was what was photographed and already discussed.
>
> **Q:** And did you have some information that there were diamonds in a cup in the house that were missing?
>
> **A:** I had received information to that effect but I wasn't able to substantiate it.

Finally, defense counsel drilled down on simple math, trying to make the point that the mileage on the diesel truck didn't align with a round-trip between Duck Creek, Utah and Conway, Arkansas during the weekend of May 18, assuming the truck was up and running. Barrett conceded, as he had to, that at an April 25, 2002 standard maintenance check, the mileage on the diesel truck was 40,211, and at the May 20, 2002 clutch service at Lunt Motors, the mileage was 42,961. That meant mileage logged between those two service events, a period of almost a month of use, was 2,750. The round trip between Duck Creek, Utah, and 6 Shady Valley in Conway, by my rough calculations, was about 2,725 miles, virtually the same, without accounting for other usage of the truck during those four weeks.

Defense counsel left it there for the time being. But it loomed as a major evidentiary issue. I knew we hadn't had our last lesson in mileage calculations.

22

THE NEXT PHASE WAS FORENSIC evidence. Apart from not being up for technical and scientific mumbo jumbo, I wasn't crazy about getting pelted with a steady stream of blood and other gruesome details. The defense and I were in similar boats; we each wanted to limit the information, they to minimize jury impact and I the personal impact. Strange bedfellows indeed.

First up was Phillip Rains, a forensic serologist with the Arkansas State Crime Laboratory. His expertise was dealing with blood and other sources for DNA testing such as semen and saliva. He had, of course, found nothing to implicate Conte. Prosecutors seemed to use Rains more for what he didn't find. *Clever,* I thought. So far as I could tell, prosecutors were recasting the absence of direct evidence as a plus, to show how Conte had learned to kill and leave a perplexing whodunnit mystery in his wake. The subtle implication was that the lack of direct evidence led straight to Conte. He had hatched what he thought was a fool-proof plan. Implicitly at least, the prosecution had turned criminal trial expectations on their head, transforming the lack of evidence into compelling evidence of guilt. Less was not always less.

Mary Robnett followed Mr. Rains. She was the CODIS Administrator for the State of Arkansas at the Arkansas State Crime Lab. CODIS—the Combined DNA Index System—is a computerized program designed to house DNA profiles from convicted offenders and arrestees, among others. She specialized in DNA. She was of a piece with Rains. She didn't add much by way of specifics, except to explain why investigators were unable to find any DNA at the crime scene: "Sometimes there's just not enough contact to leave enough DNA for us to find it and that's one of the main reasons we don't."

Again, Conte left invisible footprints all over the place.

Next came Shantell Taylor who, as it turned out, had made a finding that probably seemed curious only to me. Taylor was a criminologist in the Trace Evidence Section of the Arkansas State Crime Laboratory. Her job mainly was to "analyze hairs, fibers, paint, glass, gunshot residue, ignitable liquids, and other particles for identification."

She first testified to what we all knew. The holes in the towels "were consistent with close contact range." But what she said next blew me away.

First, some background.

My initial and visceral reaction to the news of my father's death was to think of Conte. At the start of the investigation, I urged investigators to run a vacuum cleaner through the house. I explained that Conte—who would not be on their radar until the kidnapping—had two dogs, Molly and Mickey, and in my experience, he never, and I mean never, went anywhere without them. If Conte was the perpetrator, he most likely brought the dogs for company. The vacuuming turned up nothing and I assume the exercise pushed Conte further from the suspect radar.

During his direct examination, however, Lt. Barrett testified he found a leather glove on the adjacent neighbor's property. The prosecution asked him about it, not because the glove seemed relevant of itself, but to show the jury how diligent investigators sometimes collect evidence that later is deemed unimportant. The glove testimony was a big ho-hum.

Shantell Taylor, however, tested the glove for fibers. It lacked fingerprints, interestingly enough. But it had a fiber she identified as belonging to an animal species. Was it a dog hair? What was the dog species?

Then Taylor slammed the door shut: "So animal or human, if it's animal hair then we generally don't go any farther than that unless there is something specific to do." Translation: "we weren't told to be alert to animal hairs and thus didn't test further."

I knew the odds of an incriminatory animal fiber were long. But I hoped I was wrong: if there was a match, it would be a zinger, direct evidence that placed Conte at the scene and sealed his fate.

The next forensic expert was Steve Hargis. Among other things, Hargis performed tests on firearms for the Arkansas State Crime Laboratory. He confirmed the negative, that none of the weapons or barrels seized from Conte were a ballistics match with the bullets found at the scene. It was another preemptive strike and a way of saying Conte is trying to fool you, as exemplified by what happened next.

Q: If these firearms were used with a different barrel, would it change the marks on the bullets?

A: Yes. You can change out the barrels on firearms and the new barrel may or may not have different characteristics, class characteristics, if it was made by the manufacturer.

Q: How easy is it to change barrels?

A: Someone who has no familiarity with firearms—I would not expect them to know how to change out a barrel.

By this time, the jury knew about Conte's advanced facility with firearms. They also had heard he'd trained with a SWAT team in Nevada. They knew about his weapons arsenal and that he studied military techniques. The implication was clear.

Hargis also said that the tested weapons had projectiles consistent with the use of Glaser Safety Slugs and .9mm Luger caliber safety slugs.

Q: Did they have the same amount of the characteristics, lands and grooves, and the same twist?

A: Yes. The class characteristics agreed.

Q: What are some reasons you might find the same class characteristics but not the individual characteristics?

A: It may be a different firearm barrel of the same class characteristics. It may be through the same firearm barrel and just did not either pick up the markings, or may have been damaged by passing through the target.

Q: So 'inconclusive' doesn't mean they weren't, it just means that you didn't have the individual markings to tell?

A: There's insufficient agreement of individual characteristics to identify or eliminate it.

Q: Would it have been a relatively simple matter to put a new barrel in?

A: Yes, sir. A new barrel could be easily installed.

While the ballistic results were inconclusive (but not negative), prosecutors had effectively made the point a second time that Conte may have changed out the barrels.

But the defense had not had its turn. In my conference room down the hall, I envisioned Conte whispering in the ear of his attorney, educating him on firearm barrels, as he, the expert, could do. I could imagine his attorney nodding, absorbing the information thoughtfully before rising to conduct his cross-examination. But if that happened, the jury saw it—and wondered.

Defense counsel asked Hargis to focus on the H&K firearm, the weapon that prosecutors argued Conte used to commit two murders.

Q: Can you change out the barrel on this?

A: No, sir. I believe these barrels on the Heckler & Kochs are held in place by a pin.

Q: So it's permanently in place?

A: You could remove it, but you're going to need more specialized tooling in the form of a shop press.

Q: Thank you.

Needing a specialized tool to change the barrel of the H&K complicated things. Investigators obviously didn't discover the tool in the Conte cabin, although if a juror were inclined to believe Conte tossed the barrels into the Arkansas River, it wouldn't take a leap to assume he did the same with the tool.

But how long would the barrel change take with a tool? How conspicuous would Conte be, off to the side of the road? I had no idea. Nor, I suspect, did anyone on the jury. On the other hand, he would have practiced the change before trekking to Conway. He'd have the mechanics and timing down. If you assumed Conte had planned this to a T, the H&K barrel change theory remained viable.

But it was uncertain, and that is what the defense wanted. The more questions jurors had to ask, the more deliberation debate the questions birthed, and greater the number of dots the jury had to connect—thus the greater the prospects for doubt.

The defense had again put points on the board during the prosecution's case.

23

PROSECUTORS NEXT CALLED JACK BOGARD, my high school classmate. Jack was a fellow prison inmate of Conte who'd manage to construct a heady rap sheet as a repeat offender. It appeared his legal troubles began after a three-year stint in the military. Unlike Conte and his make-believe world, Jack actually served his country.

Jack met Conte in the medical unit of the local jail where they sometimes played cards together. At first, Conte played things close to the vest, content for Jack to engage in extensive monologues, which suited the chatty Bogard fine. But that eventually changed.

Q: At first, did Conte share much with you?
A: No.
Q: Did that change over time?
A: Yeah, after I realized who he was and what he was charged with.
Q: What do you mean?
A: Well, when I said, "You're the guy accused of killing Carter Elliott."
Q: Did he respond?
A: He said he was.

Q: Did you know who Carter Elliott was?

A: Yes, Ashley's dad.

Q: Did you know any of the details of the case or facts of the case other than Carter Elliott was killed?

A: That was the only thing I knew, and that it was years ago.

Q: Once you realized he was the person charged with killing Carter Elliott, what did you say to him and what did he respond?

A: He asked me if I knew Ashley and I said yeah, and he elaborated on how much he hated her and how big of a bitch she was.

Q: Did he use that word?

A: He did.

Q: Did you ask him anything else?

A: Yes. I asked him straight out, "Did you do it?"

Q: What did he say in response?

A: The man said, "Hell, yeah, but they have no evidence."

Q: Did he elaborate about the lack of evidence?

A: He did. He said they didn't have a murder weapon and would never have one, that they tested the wrong vehicle for bugs, that they were running out of time, and he'd be free soon.

Q: Did he say anything about a second victim?

A: He did. He referred to him as the bodyguard.

I tried to visualize this exchange. Did Conte flash gloating eyes when he fessed up? Was his tone as boastful as his words? Did he speak matter-of-factly, as if it were no big deal? And what went through his mind? Did he have any sense of what he did to my family at this point? Were we to him mere collateral damage, like Timmy Wayne? Did he have any guilt or remorse? Did the killings lift Conte from the doldrums of his self-pity of unrequited love? Did bragging about the killings pump life into his banty rooster complex?

Would we ever find the answers or would they and others die with him?

Bogard also testified that in admitting the crime, Conte explained he did it "over Carter's ex-wife" and that my mother "wanted [my father] dead." Was he implying my mother helped plan the murders or directed him to do what he did?

I didn't buy either. I could see my mother making a sloppy comment out of frustration, like the asinine comment Kevin Clark made at Chow's restaurant the year before. And I could see how such a comment might fuel Conte's homicidal cause to win my mother back. But I could not see a conspiracy between the two of them, even though in the early days of the investigation, I confessed to dark thoughts about possible family complicity.

The brazen comment about my mother to Bogard was typical Conte, his way of justifying what he did, casting blame elsewhere.

But the confession rang true. It was consistent with the Conte boastful side. His dominant flaw, the part of him that rotted his soul, was his unyielding fondness for fantasizing about himself, making up things to impress people and improve his social standing.

The confession also spoke to the wisdom of filing charges early and not waiting, underscoring what I at least perceived as the misguided discretion of former prosecutors who had sat idle. Even I could see that a looming capital murder trial, where your life is on the line, can trigger all sorts of things, including the loosening of the tongue. It harkened to the advice someone gave Foster in the earlier goings, which I am told he rejected out of hand: that the prospects of the life imprisonment or the death penalty easily could bring Conte to the bargaining table to make a deal. It wasn't precisely the same situation, but it housed the same dynamic of cause and effect that eluded former prosecutors. Hold Conte's feet to the fire and good things will come. It's a shame the old protectors of the people seemed not to understand that much.

The prosecution looked to wrap it up with Jack Bogard.

Q: Did you decide to do anything with what you learned from Conte?

A: Yes.

Q: Tell the jury, please, what you did and why.

A: I sent a letter to Trey Elliott to let him know what I learned.

Q: Why?

A: I started thinking about the whole situation and I said to myself, 'if that was my father, I would want someone to help me,' so I wrote him a letter.

Bogard also confirmed that the prosecution hadn't offered him anything in exchange for his testimony and that his testimony was not a ploy to curry favor with district attorney's office, which he described as "coming after him."

The defense predictably tried to discredit Bogard with his extensive criminal record, mostly drugs and petty theft. Bogard conceded, "drugs have destroyed my life." The defense also tried to discredit Bogard with the barrage of letters he wrote months before the trial, admittedly hunting for a prosecutorial deal. Bogard acknowledged he'd love some help but was consistently clear prosecutors wouldn't budge.

Jack sounded sincere. He didn't get defensive when he got a defense counsel tongue-lashing about his criminal past and efforts to get favorable treatment. He wasn't evasive, either. He was polite, respectful, and straightforward. He came off trying to do the right thing.

After Bogard returned to his prison cell, Joey Gray, a fellow inmate, replaced him in the witness box. The prosecution took Gray through the same paces of his extensive criminal record and pending charges. They also took great pains to show Gray didn't have a deal and that the prosecutor's office had been hard on him.

Gray was a self-described "book reader type." He didn't play cards and he never interacted with Conte. He shared space with Conte in the medical pod, a day room with four beds, while receiving attention for a broken arm. It was then he overheard the conversation between Bogard and Conte. Here is Gray's account.

Q: Was there one day when you saw Jack and the defendant playing cards alone?

A: Yes, ma'am.

Q: Did you overhear them having a conversation?

A: Yeah. They conversated every time. But that particular day it was a different conversation.

Q: How was it different?

A: They was just talking about their cases.

Q: Did you hear Jack ask Dick Conte something about his case?

A: Jack was always talking about how it was going in his case. I think that was the first thing that was said. And Conte said they didn't have nothing on him.

Q: What else did Conte say?

A: He mentioned an Ashley, who he had a lot of animosity towards for some reason, like she was the reason he was in this mess.

Q: What else?

A: I guess it got towards the end and Jack said "Well, did you do it?"

Q: How did Conte answer?

A: He said, "Yeah, I did, but they ain't got no proof."

Gray added that he never approached prosecutors; they approached him. He also mentioned that Jack Bogard was upset about Conte's confession because Jack knew the victim's family. The prosecution closed their direct of Gray with this:

Q: You don't know any of the victims involved in this case?

A: No.

Q: Tell this jury why you're here, then. Because this can't be a comfortable place for you.

A: Because if it was my father, I'd want someone, if they knew anything, to come forward. That's why I'm here. Because I've lost my father and I could feel that family's loss, you know.

After the prosecution "passed the witness," the defense did what little it could do, spending virtually their entire time on Gray's criminal record, which included two prison escapes that resulted in capture and more jail time, as well as his pending legal problems. They avoided the confession he overheard. I felt, again, the defense failed to undermine the truthfulness of what Gray said he overheard.

The cumulative effect of the Bogard and Gray testimony struck me as significant, like a final nail in the coffin. But I had to ask: did I believe what I wanted to believe? Was I reacting like a member of a choir hearing the welcome words of an admired pastor?

I had to wonder whether some jurors might turn deaf ears to whatever Jack Bogard and Joey Gray had to say. The two played by different rules than the law-abiding citizens of the jury, fashioning a lifestyle that skirted the law to get whatever they wanted. Could they be trusted? Could they sell snake oil with a straight face? On the other hand, both seemed almost charming and humble. Despite nervousness, their voices radiated honesty.

What about the fact they violated the unwritten prison code against snitching? Which way did that cut? Bogard admitted he was taking a risk by testifying, but said he drew a line on the unwritten code when it came to murder, rape and child molestation, a high road I hoped would resonate with the jury. Further, both testified to a moral imperative, helping the family, Bogard because he knew us and Gray because he'd lost his father, too. That counted for something, it seemed to me.

And what about prosecutorial credibility? Faulkner County was for the most part conservative. Would jurors assume that prosecutors only put truthful witnesses in front of them? Did each juror have an abiding belief in the fairness of the criminal justice system? Or were those naïve assumptions?

More than ever, I wanted to be inside the minds of jurors after Gray left the stand. But I remained offstage, in a continuous limbo state, like getting teased with movie trailers but denied the chance to watch the entire feature film.

The show was far from over, though. The prosecution had one more witness before turning the case over to the defense, and that was

Dr. Stephen Erickson, the Chief Medical Examiner for the State of Arkansas. Erickson oversaw determinations of the cause and manner of death of individuals who have died in violent circumstances.

Before Erickson took the stand, the judge issued a warning to the assembled multitudes:

"There are pictures which will be presented to this jury that some may find hard to look at. If you are in that category and you do not believe that you can maintain your seat and not react in an inappropriate manner, you may stay. If you feel like you're going to be bothered by that, now would be the time to leave."

I wondered whether I was the poster child for that admonition.

Erickson described his work as building a story from gunshot wounds, a grisly form of event reconstruction. His testimony was painfully specific even without the autopsy photos, which I had no interest in ever seeing. It was, again, a time to appreciate my courtroom exile. I couldn't see how the jurors could sit through the Erickson testimony and not be repulsed. The only piece of relative comfort was knowing that my father and Timmy Wayne died instantaneously or, as Erickson put it, with immediate "complete stillness and unresponsiveness."

Erickson topped off his contributions by testifying, over vigorous defense objections, that my father and Timmy Wayne were "under the control of" the perpetrator "at the time of their death," and there was "purpose to end their lives" through "execution."

The Erickson testimony enflamed my hate for Conte so much, it frightened me. His crimes, continued arrogance, and seeming indifference to the pain and suffering he'd caused, tested me to the limits. Calling him a despicable human being was charitable.

The defense did little with Erickson, other than a meek attempt to narrow the gap about time of death, which seemed to go nowhere.

Then the prosecution rested.

As I suspect is standard, the Court heard and denied the expected defense motions for a directed verdict that sought dismissal of the case, finding that that the prosecution had made out a *prima facie* case for conviction.

The prosecution had built a conviction case in increments, each building on the other, brick by brick, leading to the jailhouse confessions and the grand finale, the gruesomely graphic reminders of why the jury was called to civic duty. It was far from perfect. The lack of direct evidence cast a long shadow. But it was solid. How would the defense respond?

24

THE DEFENSE PUT ON A relatively short case. They had in spots leveraged the prosecution's case in chief to inflict what damage they could, and by this time had only a few points to make. They called several witnesses but only three seemed central and, as I saw it, they produced mixed results at best.

It started with a skirmish over whether the Court should allow testimony from two representatives of the company Alan Duke hired to clean my dad's home early on May 20.

The prosecution argued that the testimony would be unfairly prejudicial in light of Lt. Barrett's testimony that investigators released the house to the family early that morning. The point was that the family could do what it wanted with the home once investigators were done, and whatever happened afterward didn't impact the prior evidence gathering.

The defense countered that the jury should be allowed to determine whether a hasty turnover and cleanup compromised evidence, including fingerprints, which, if so, tainted the investigation. Disallowing the testimony, they argued, unfairly prejudiced Conte.

It was a battle of the unfair prejudices.

The Court sided with the defense but imposed limitations that in turn prompted the defense to withdraw one of the two witnesses.

That left Jeff Beebe, who specialized in "disaster restoration." An admittedly nervous Beebe understandably had a fuzzy memory of what happened in 2002. But he remembered enough to move the needle for the defense.

Beebe recalled that Alan Duke urgently wanted the place cleaned the morning of May 20. Duke directed him to remove carpet and clean anything that might have "blood or fingerprint dust," which included staircase handrails, door casings, doors, and the foyer floors. He testified it was unusual to clean up crime scenes with police still on the site, as there were here, and with yellow caution tape hugging the property perimeter, as was the case as well. And he distinctly remembered refusing to comply with Duke's odd request that Beebe remove the yellow tape.

While not a blockbuster moment, the defense had raised suspicion about what drove the urgency to cleanse the crime scene—although nothing suggested law enforcement had a hand in the cleanup timing—and about possible destruction of evidence, especially fingerprints.

I had wondered for years why Duke wanted to bum-rush a cleanup, especially since back then I included him in my short list of murder suspects. Now, with the benefit of substantial hindsight, I saw how the rushed cleaning might have made sense, as family members were soon to gather at the home that day. Duke, sadly, died several months before the trial and so presumably we'll never know his state of mind.

I assumed as well that the Conway PD and FBI teams had dusted adequately for fingerprints, gathering what they could. Until this point in the trial, nothing so much as hinted that the investigation was anything but thorough, including with the collection of prints.

Still, despite the impression they were clutching at straws, the defense had at least managed to tee up questions without answers, an apparent defense formula for doubt. Hopefully, the jury would deem them unworthy of their attention.

The defense also called Nate Hindman, a firearms expert. He had little to say about the specific evidence in the case and gave more of a tutorial on why the type of weaponry involved here was not unique and commonly found in many places. On cross-examination, however, prosecutors teased concessions from him.

Hindman affirmed that novice firearm owners normally don't possess the Blue Tip Glaser Safety Slug rounds, which was typically the province of firearm collectors. Blue Tip slugs are so expensive and functionally specialized, they never are used for target practice. They are designed and used to cause great harm, "to disperse all of its energy into the target rather than pass through it" and cause maximum internal damage within a "controlled setting." He confirmed that the damage depicted in the crime scene photos was consistent with use of the Glaser slugs.

He acknowledged, too, that the barrels of a "standard .9mm handgun," like used in this case, are easily changed, even by a "novice" using an "instruction booklet." And, when asked about firearm barrels that are more difficult to change, he said: "any competent person that works on firearms may have the tools or ability to change a barrel out."

The prosecution had skillfully turned Hindman into our witness and the defense, by calling him as an expert, had shot itself in the foot.

The defense then called Jackson Cabell, a "trucking industry" expert, with a concentration on "mileage and distance calculations." I assumed Cabell was the defense's ace in the hole.

The defense had asked Cabell to perform three calculations of mileage and driving time, using three different itineraries. His work assumed a constant driving speed of 65 miles an hour, no stopping, and 2002 driving conditions. Cabell employed three calculation methodologies for each of the three itineraries. The first was the "PC miler," an industry computer program set up for trucks. The other two were the MapQuest and Google distance programs.

The first itinerary was Carson City, Nevada to Conway, Arkansas to Duck Creek, Utah:

3,316.50 miles and 51.46 driving hours.

3,283.60 miles and 49.5 driving hours

3,227 miles and 48 driving hours

The second was Carson City to Duck Creek to Conway to Duck Creek:

3,476 miles and 54.02 hours

3,387 miles and 52 hours

3,286 miles and 51 hours

The third was Duck Creek to Conway to Duck Creek:

2,829 miles and 43.20 hours

2,882 miles and 42.5 hours

2,721 miles and 42 hours

The defense was trying to stack the deck. Nothing in the case indicated Conte traveled other than from Utah to Arkansas and back.

For one, it was clear that if he was the guy, he returned from Conway directly to Duck Creek. Phone records showed he called my mother from Duck Creek at 9:59 p.m. Sunday May 19. For two, phone records showed he used the Utah landline on May 16. Three, his alibi witness, Mr. Pringle, purportedly saw him driving the truck in Utah over the weekend in Duck Creek, where Pringle lived.

The defense's attempt to toss up an amalgam of mileage and driving time numbers for other itineraries was classic smokescreen.

Cabell also testified about the diesel truck odometer readings, using the earlier discussed service records on April 25 and May 20, 2002. He testified that, for the approximately four-week period between the two maintenance service visits, the odometer showed 2,748 miles. He then confirmed the obvious: the mileage was substantially less than what was contained in the first two sets of calculations. Revealingly, defense counsel didn't ask him to do the math for the third itinerary calculations. That omission seemed glaring—if the jury used the third itinerary, the mileage theory was a complete bust. He then passed the witness.

The prosecution established that the speed limits on the basic route, Interstate 40, for all three itineraries ranged from 70 to 80 miles per hour, which Cabell acknowledged meant the trip could be made in "significantly" less time than if driving 65 miles per hour, the benchmark he used. He conceded it could mean a three- to four-hour difference. So, for example, using the third itinerary the defense ignored, the round trip from Utah to Arkansas could be made in 39 hours—about 20 hours each way—assuming no stopping. It was a vigorous trip to be sure, but doable.

It was more about the last leg of the trip. Conte easily could have left for Conway on May 17. But the back end, from Conway to Duck Creek, bracketed a tighter time frame. If Conte left Conway on May 18 around 11 p.m., which I believed was likely, he'd have about 23 hours driving time available, more than enough time to dump the barrels, make a pit stop or two, and be comfortably at Duck Creek to call my mother at 9:59 p.m. on May 19.

Would the array of calculations confuse the jury? Would jurors be sufficiently comfortable with the tight time frame and be inclined to number crunch meticulously? If their opinions were pretty much etched in stone by this point, would they even care?

The prosecution also got Cabell to acknowledge that diesel trucks make "several unique noises" "louder" than what gasoline-powered vehicles emit. This was another out-of-the-blue question that sailed over my head. I would, however, later appreciate its significance.

After Cabell stepped down from the stand, the defense requested a recess to confer with Conte about testifying. I prayed it would happen. It'd be fitting for him to sit up there, under oath, and justify his wasted existence. If they called him, I was prepared to lobby hard for my return to the courtroom, like a Prodigal Daughter.

Fifteen minutes later, Conte and his attorneys returned to the courtroom. Conte told the Court he declined to testify, acknowledging that he "freely and voluntarily" and "without any coercion, promises, threats," elected his Fifth Amendment right against self-incrimination. The prospects had been too good to be true.

The defense rested and the prosecution declined any rebuttal.

After the Court denied the customary spate of defense motions, all that remained was instructions to the jury on the law, closing arguments, jury deliberations—and hopefully, justice.

I was free to reenter the courtroom. I eagerly awaited closing arguments.

25

THE PROSECUTION'S CLOSING ARGUMENT ZEROED in on one central theme: the circumstantial evidence was too abundant and systematic to constitute anything but a motive-directed, painstakingly constructed, and purposeful criminal plan. The evidence told a tale that triggered flashbacks of a time I was more than ready to leave behind. I hoped the jury could transport themselves in time with me, to see what I saw and feel what I and my family felt and went through.

The story I heard boiled down to this: Conte's criminal purpose developed over several months like a snowball cascading into an avalanche and culminating in wanton destruction.

When my mother left Conte, he literally broke down, weeping and begging her not to leave him. He was uncontrollably distraught. He responded by showering her with an embarrassing bevy of gifts and love messages, sending as many as one hundred cards in an attempt to reignite her feelings. He made it painfully clear he wasn't going quietly into the night.

His over-the-top romantic offerings, however, landed with a big thud. My mother was not turning back.

Undeterred, he reached deeper into his wacko bag, contriving an insane story about taking sniper fire in Afghanistan, all the while expressing his undying love for my mother, only to return from the faux battlefield to brandish phony bullet wounds. It was as bizarre a gambit to rekindle affection imaginable. And it revealed more than agonizing unrequited love: it betrayed his sociopathic tendencies.

Like the futile romance barrage, the mercenary play didn't help his cause. On the contrary. It pushed my mother further away, strengthened her resolve, and reaffirmed the wisdom of her decision to end the relationship.

I drifted here to wonder whether something specifically triggered Conte and sent him over the edge, spiraling him into sheer madness. For several months, he was head deep in a reclamation project to win back my mother. But at least by May 11, 2002, when he downloaded Conway maps and radio frequencies, he had devised a more demonic plan. How and when did he decide that my father stood in his way? Then I remembered something.

We had heard during the investigation that the FBI was pursuing a lead that Conte may have been on site at my engagement party on April 13, five weeks before the murders, spying from a distance, probably using military grade binoculars. If that were true, he got an alarming visual of my parents carrying on in the parking lot like teenagers in heat at the end of the festivities. But apparently the FBI never confirmed the rumor, certainly it never came up during the trial, even though the shoe fit exceedingly well. Perhaps instead he learned about the frolicking from his pal, my Uncle Kevin, who attended the wedding, when the two met to remove the faux bullets shortly after Conte returned from his fantasy trip to Afghanistan on April 17. The timing worked and I could see Conte getting an earful about how well my parents got along at the party. What might have seemed harmless banter to my uncle could have ignited Conte's imagination that my parents had been carrying on for months, which was the reason my mother dumped him. Perhaps. And who knows to what extent my mother expressed feelings about my father as a defensive device to ward off Conte's juggernaut of advances.

In all events . . . .

The divorce then became final. The writing, literally, was on the wall. From Conte's standpoint, his life lay in the balance. He had to win my mother back. No extreme was too far.

Whatever the dynamics, in his mind, Conte began to see my father as a threat he had to eliminate.

His malicious plan was meticulous. He had the means and the know-how. He had the bases covered. He was smarter than the rest of us. He wouldn't leave anything traceable to himself. He would confound the world with the perfect crime.

So he killed for love—if that's what you want to call it.

But the murders didn't move the romantic needle, bringing Conte deep despair. He was at his wits' end, truly desperate.

So he furthered his irrational crusade by kidnapping my mother. He planned a murder-suicide, his version of "if he can't have her" warped thinking. But for some reason, he abandoned the plan and surrendered. His spirit was deflated.

The prosecution didn't mention the underlying force in this saga: down deep, in the dark recesses of Conte's psyche, my mother was his life savior, the cure for his perpetual torment as a lonely, insecure, loveless, and miserable person. He saw in her the ultimate fix to make his life right, give him the instant respectability he had always wanted, something his mercenary fantasies tried to serve but never adequately could. My mother was his depraved version of a trophy wife.

So when she cut him loose, he couldn't deal. His life, at bottom, was over, and he went on a path of destruction. Everything he did along that dark and unseemly road was designed to reclaim his life.

He had motive to spare.

As the prosecution pointed out, Conte told my mother he would do anything to win her back. I am sure she never imagined how literally he meant that.

There were many other details in the closing argument. The prosecution talked about Pringle, the use of the Jeep instead of the diesel truck, the photos of my father in his cabin, the internet searches for radio frequencies and local street maps, the phone records, the weaponry, and so on. They were important details. But the story I heard and envisioned, and prayed that the jury absorbed, was the story I'd lived. Prosecutors dubbed it "Conte's final recon mission."

The defense tried hard to take the air out the prosecutorial balloon. By trial time, the prosecution had figured out that Conte used the Jeep during the round trip, either by itself or towed by the diesel truck. That explained why the defense tried so hard to keep the still shot of the truck towing the Jeep out of evidence. They knew the truth. They played along with the trap Conte had set. They knew the lies they were peddling about the diesel truck and tried to get everyone to focus on a phony set of facts.

The defense argued there was no evidence of the Jeep stored at Duck Creek. That mystified me because it is precisely what the photo showed—both vehicles parked at Duck Creek. Besides, how easy would it be to tow the Jeep from Carson City, Nevada, the site of the kidnapping, to Utah? Pretty easy, I think.

Further, as Bogard and Gray testified, Conte boasted that investigators tested the wrong truck. That wasn't something the papers reported. There was no way either witness could have made that up. Conte said it for sure, in a moment of arrogant bluster. He essentially admitted he used the Jeep for part or all of the round-trip journey.

The defense did the mileage math again, focusing solely on the two longer itineraries but not the most likely of the three, Utah to Arkansas to Utah. Classic strawman argument.

The defense also spent significant time trying to undermine the credibility of Bogard and Gray. The defense maligned the two of them as "terrible citizens" and "thieves" who were "not worthy of belief" and who wanted to steal again, this time robbing trust from the jury.

But most of all, the defense focused on the legal standard of reasonable doubt and, in that context, how all the holes in the evidence created too much uncertainty and required too much a leap of faith to convict Conte of the serious offense of capital murder.

The defense thus pounded hard on its central theme of the case, that the prosecution was all about "speculation and conjecture." They harped on the facts that nobody testified Conte did those awful things, and he was in Arkansas when the crimes occurred. They emphasized the lack of evidence that any hostility existed between Conte and my father, or they'd ever had a "dustup." They reminded the jury my mother said Conte never expressed any ill-will toward my father and she had never wanted any harm to come to him. And of course, they highlighted the absence of DNA, fingerprints, and a murder weapon.

I imagine that in all criminal cases, no matter what the quality of the evidence, the most powerful weapon the defense has is the legal standard of reasonable doubt. Jurors had to be sure, real sure, before they made a decision that sent someone to prison. And not most of the jurors. Every one of them.

Here was the defense's most plaintive plea:

"Don't let them lure you down this path of guessing what happened. We don't convict people in our system of justice based on the possibility somebody did something."

Those words struck me hard and invoked fear. I thought, *We're fucked! There is no way they're going to find him guilty!*

Despite the prosecution's clever and effective handling of the evidence and witnesses, they were unable to reconstruct the crime itself. They didn't have the evidence. They didn't have it because it didn't exist. Conte had planned well enough to leave gaping potholes all over the most important path of the storyline.

Opinions about how it happened existed, including variations from Lt. Jim Barrett, the lead investigator, and Special Agent Jerry Spurgers, who oversaw the FBI part of the investigation. But opinions about the facts, no matter how well-considered and persuasive, aren't shared with the jury. Would jurors have their own projections of what went down? Would their reconstruction of events go something like the following?

Conte left Duck Creek around midnight on Friday, May 17 driving his red Jeep. He didn't take the diesel truck for two reasons. One, its distinctly noisy engine would attract attention and, two, the disabled diesel truck was an investigative trap he'd set for law enforcement. He knew that if he became a person of interest or a suspect, investigators would focus on the diesel truck, his main form of transportation.

The open question: what did he do with the two dogs?

He pulled up to 6 Shady Valley about 10:30 p.m. He was wearing a black SWAT team uniform, a Kevlar vest, helmet, badge, ski mask or a balaclava (found at Conte's place later), and his signature boots. He was carrying an H&K 94 9mm rifle and a SIG Sauer P220 handgun with a suppressor. He had white towels he purchased from Walmart in his pockets.

He knocked hard on the door and announced himself as police with a search warrant. Both my father and Timmy Wayne were watching television and thought it was a friendly prank. They were stunned to see law enforcement in the doorway.

Conte directed them to lie down, face first, and put their hands around their backs so he could cuff them. They obeyed without more ado.

Many people believe that neither man would lie down without a fight. Facing a well-armed member of law enforcement, however, they had little option but to submit. Better to cooperate and resolve misunderstandings another time.

I'm guessing my father said, "What's this all about?" In response, Conte probably said, "Be quiet and still," and then, standing near Timmy Wayne, Conte racked the slide of the handgun back to make a noise that conveys, "Don't fuck with me. I mean business." When he did, an unfired round popped out of the chamber and landed inside Timmy Wayne's cap.

Conte grabbed the towels to control blood spatter, and which in addition to the suppressor would muffle sound. He put the towel in place and shot Timmy Wayne once, and then did the same to my father, using the H&K 94 .9mm firearm.

Before leaving, Conte wanted to leave signs of a robbery. He grabbed a knife out of his pocket and tore the left back pocket of my father's jeans to look as if the perpetrator had searched for a wallet.

Conte policed the used H&K rounds, but in the darkness of the foyer, he couldn't find the unfired round from the handgun. Not wanting to delay his exit, he left the round at the scene.

It was 11 p.m. when he made his way back. He had previously identified a place along Interstate 40 to access the Arkansas River, probably near Russellville, Arkansas. Once there, he removed the barrels from both weapons and inserted them into a bag he had filled with heavy metal. He tossed the bag into the river and resumed his trip to Duck Creek, doped with amphetamine to keep him alert.

He arrived in Duck Creek, in the vicinity of 9 p.m. Mountain time. Once settled in, he replaced the tossed barrels, wiped down his boots, threw his clothes into the wash, cleaned down the knife (unless he tossed that, too, into the river), and at 9:59 p.m. placed a call on his landline to my mother, the one person he'd want to know what he'd done but couldn't tell. He didn't reach her. Three minutes later, at 10:02 p.m., he called his mother in Wisconsin.

The Court excused the jury to deliberate at 3:25 p.m., I hung around the courtroom before heading home, but I never got the chance to leave. Fifty-four minutes later, at 4:19 p.m., we received word the jury had concluded its deliberations and reached a verdict.

26

MY HEART SKIPPED A FEW beats on the news the jury had made up its collective mind in less than an hour. I was stunned. I had little doubt it struck others the same way. Most everyone, including media, were still hanging around, stragglers like me chit-chatting in the halls and parking lot.

I didn't have a good feeling.

A caravan of interested parties meandered toward the courtroom, emitting a low buzz of anticipation. As I neared the courtroom, a prosecutor pulled me aside to instruct me how to act: I was not to look at anybody; I was to keep my eyes down; I was to show no emotion on the reading of the verdicts; and I for sure was not "to make any faces."

Really? What if I shed a tear? Or two? Will they exile me again? Unbelievable.

Of all the exasperating things I had experienced in more than a decade of this process, to be told to act like a mannequin when I was about to hear whether a jury had concluded someone had murdered my father was, hands down, the lowest blow of them all.

It was dehumanizing.

I could see how criminal justice practitioners get jaded over time, how emotional survival and effective advocacy require deep detachment from the human elements of the experience. But when the work deadens your heart and robs you of basic empathy, well, to my way of living, you've lost your way. You've traded in your core humanity.

Surely the system can tolerate a few tears. Surely common decency has a place in the criminal justice process.

I didn't respond to the condescension. I had plenty to handle with my swelling anxiety about an impending verdict. I walked into the courtroom, joining my close friend, Stephanie, inside.

The judge emerged to take the bench. People rose on cue, and the sound of a full courtroom, except for wheelchair-bound Conte, rising and retaking seats in unison, gave off a resounding *swoosh*. The courtroom then went pin-drop silent as we waited for the ceremonial entry of the keepers of fate. I focused on harnessing the wild energy inside my brain.

The side door creaked open and the jury shuffled in. Most had their heads tilted down. They didn't look at anyone. They were somber.

The judge nodded to jury foreman Billy Jackson, who rose slowly and passed the verdict slips to the clerk who relayed them to the judge. The judge peered at the slips and slightly nodded his head. His face revealed nothing. Good poker face.

My body tightened. I looked down and released a long breath. I closed my eyes. The anticipation was sheer torment. The judge then spoke.

> **The Court:** "All right, sir. I have verdicts that read, first: 'In the matter of Carter Elliott, we, the jury, find Richard Conte guilty of capital murder,' which bears your signature. Is that your verdict, sir?"
>
> **Mr. Jackson:** "Yes, sir."

I didn't budge. I kept my eyes shut and down. My heart raced. I wanted to scream.

The Court, reading: "In the matter of Carter Elliott, do you, the jury, find 'beyond a reasonable doubt that Richard Conte employed a firearm as a means of capital murder.' You have checked yes with your signature. Is that your verdict?"
Mr. Jackson: "Yes, Your Honor."

I could hear my heart pounding. I wondered if others could, too. Was it permissible for my heart to pound loudly, prosecutors? I squeezed Stephanie's hand. I wanted to peek at Conte. I dared not.

The Court: "Okay. 'With regard to Timmy Wayne Robertson, we, the jury, find Richard Conte guilty of capital murder' with your signature. Is that your verdict?"
Mr. Jackson: "Yes, Your Honor."

I controlled my breathing. It was going to be a sweep. It was about to be over. My God.

The Court: And "do you, the jury, find 'beyond a reasonable doubt that Richard Conte employed a firearm as a means of committing capital murder?' You checked yes with your signature. Is that your verdict, sir?"
Mr. Jackson: "Yes, Your Honor."
The Court: "Very well, thank you. Anybody require anything of this panel?"

The defense asked the judge to "poll the jury," meaning each juror, one at a time, had to affirm their assent to the read verdict.

The Court: "I've been asked to poll the jury which means, Mr. Jackson, I'll start with you. we'll work our way down the front row. Mr. Jackson, is this your verdict?"
Mr. Jackson: "Yes, it is."

Down the line, eleven more, without equivocation, each separately affirming the verdicts. Figurative nails in a coffin. Each "It is" or "Yes, Your Honor" filled the courtroom with finality and soothed the pain in my soul.

Wow.

I didn't expect what came next.

The Court announced we had "come to the sentencing phase." I assumed this would happen months later, like it did in the Nevada kidnapping case. But Arkansas, evidently, was one of the few states that empowers the jury to pass out punishment for criminal convictions. The parties, however, may waive that right in deference to the Court doing the dirty work. The Court looked to the attorneys to see if they'd reached agreement. They had. Both waived sentencing by the jury, putting the onus squarely on the judge who wasted not a second.

"Richard Conte, in Case No. CR-2011-1028, the jury, having found you guilty of the offense of capital murder in the death of Carter Elliott, the Court will sentence you to a period of life in the Arkansas Department of Corrections.

"The jury further finding that you've used a firearm in the commission of that offense, the Court will sentence you to an additional fifteen years in the Arkansas Department of Corrections to run consecutively with that life sentence.

"The jury further having found you guilty of the offense of capital murder in the death of Timmy Wayne Robertson, the Court will sentence you to a period of life in the Arkansas Department of Corrections.

"The jury further having found that you used a firearm in the commission of that offense, the Court will sentence you to an additional fifteen years in the Arkansas Department of Corrections to run consecutively with that sentence.

"These sentences shall run consecutively with each other.

"Do you understand that sentence, sir?"

"Yes," said Conte.

"Do you have anything to say?" The Court followed.

"No."

The chatty banty rooster had nothing to say? You aren't going to treat us to some bullshit song and dance about innocence or excuse? You aren't going to stumble through some half-assed apology? You are content to hang your head? *Now* you're going quietly into the night?

He was beaten down. His life was over. I felt relieved. I know an appeal awaited. But the odds greatly favored him spending the rest of his life in jail. We had turned a corner.

The jury verdict and life sentences, however, didn't eliminate the pain of my loss, pain that I expected to last a long time. I had my own life sentence. I had internal work to do, and with family. Time would help. The rest was on me.

I went home, played some music, and danced around the house. I prayed and thanked the Lord. I spoke to my friends Stephanie, Ann, and Tami, who as always, gave me unconditional support, love, and compassion. My family members, including my Mom, got together for dinner and drinks and then, predictably, all went their separate ways.

A new phase of life had begun.

27

AFTER THE CRIMINAL TRIAL FADED to distant memory, I thought about visiting Conte in prison. I wanted answers. I wanted to know.

Each time I mentioned the idea to family and friends, I got greeted, without exception, with an adamant "no."

"You don't want to know."

"Don't do that to yourself."

"No good can come of it."

Part of me, admittedly, feared looking at him across protective prison glass. Another part yearned for what the jury verdict and his life sentence couldn't give me: I needed to understand better what happened. Even though I had my firm views, I needed, for some reason, to hear it from him and go deeper into the darkness. I needed a reckoning.

I didn't want part of any redemption project. I didn't want to connect with the perpetrator and make amends. I sure as hell didn't want to forgive. I wanted to find a better place and, yeah, get in his face and go off on him, too.

But I wasn't at a place in my life where I had the strength to overcome the powerful admonitions of others. I didn't have the emotional fortitude to be bold. So, I deferred. I don't blame anyone.

Their pushbacks were genuine desires to protect me, from the unknown and maybe myself. I tabled the idea. That was on me.

A couple of years passed. I remarried and rebuilt my life, dedicating myself to my children and husband. But I never stopped wanting answers. I felt incomplete, trapped in confusion, yearning to know. I feared I might never escape. I started therapy and worked on myself. Things got better.

Conte, however, remained a missing piece. Every now and then, the thought of visiting him slid into my consciousness. Was it too late? Do I need to do it? Then the routines and demands of everyday life would take over, and I'd move forward.

Fate took control.

In early December 2017, I was running on a treadmill when my cell phone buzzed. I recognized the number from the criminal trial. I stopped running, removed the headphones, cleared my face of sweat, and answered. It was one of the prosecuting attorneys.

"Conte is dead."

"Dead? You're kidding? Really?"

"Yeah."

"How?"

"I'm not at liberty to say."

"What? You can't tell me? Why?"

"I'm not allowed to give out that information right now. But he is dead. It's over."

Conte died on Thursday, December 7, 2017, five years after his conviction. He took his last breath in the medical ward of the Arkansas Department of Correction.

My first emotion was relief. Gone was the fear he might someday try to harm me. When he died, he had a second appeal pending before the Arkansas Supreme Court and who knew what would come of that. I had learned not to book bet on legal system outcomes. His death assured that he could never pound on my door like he did at Shady Valley on May 18, 2002. I was safe. My family was safe. Richard Ralph Conte was no longer.

His death, interestingly, didn't give me vengeful satisfaction. Yes, he was a monster who killed my father and a friend and kidnapped and assaulted my unconscious mother. Yet part of me felt sad, and I'm not sure why.

Nor was it "over," not for me. His death left a permanent hole, extinguishing any chance of finding the answers only he could provide.

I resorted to imagination.

What would it have been like seeing him again, looking him in the eyes, asking him questions? I saw myself at the Arkansas state prison, walking through security, getting pat downs, and suffering laborious prison procedures to assure I posed no risk. I imagined myself getting ushered to a secure meeting space with a protective glass, waiting for Conte to emerge and sit across from me. I imagined hearing a heavy door open and seeing a prison guard escort Conte in his wheelchair toward me.

Conte steals a peek in my direction. But once close, he averts his eyes. He looks sad. He looks defeated.

We sit in silence for thirty seconds. He shuffles in his mobile unit, trying to get more comfortable, clears his throat, and says nothing. He keeps his eyes tilted down.

I dispense with formalities like "How're ya doing?"

"Dick, it's odd. Every now and then, I see you in random places like the Atlanta Aquarium. The man I went scuba diving with looked like you and his name was Dick. It was the best dive of my life and the worst dive of my life. Remember?"

It's not a smooth start. I am uncomfortable. His eyes are still cast down.

"I think I see you sometimes at the checkout line of the market where I live out of the corner of my eye. The sight of you steals my breath. I sneak a glance to make sure it's you rather than someone who reminds me of you. I get closer, inch up behind you, hoping that you'll turn so I can confirm it is you. You turn around. It's someone else.

"You forever haunt me, with those beady eyes and beak nose, that strange voice and stooped stature, your khaki outfits, costumes you wore to look like someone you were not. And that fucking hat you used to wear. That silly stupid hat. It is always on your head when I imagine you. You looked like an overgrown, self-conscious, ill-at-ease boy scout who never grew up, always trapped in a miserable childhood, trying to find his way out awkwardly."

I lean back to gather more oxygen. He is still looking down. He is taking it. I wonder if he'll ask me to leave. Get fed up. I don't care. I continue. I feel meanness coming on.

"I sincerely tried to like you. I did. You were married to my mom, for fuck's sake. I wanted to accept you. But I couldn't. Mostly, I felt sorry for you. My mother didn't love you. Did you honestly believe she did? Didn't you know it was a game?

"Did you not know her? She liked the good things in life. You had guns and knives and combat paraphernalia and mercenary soldier stories and a redneck truck and other eerie shit. Oh, yes, you had a medical license. That counted for something.

"As soon as my mom got a close look at your life, she was out of there. Buyer's remorse. I mean, how long before the bottom fell out? Less than six months?

"I felt sorry for you when that happened. I did." I can't believe I said that, but at that point of the narrative, it was true.

I detect an ever-so-slight nod, barely perceptible, as if he is struggling to visualize what I am saying. He doesn't utter a word. I scan the area to make sure I am safe.

"I know now that my mom sent you countless emails professing her love for you. You had nicknames for each another."

He manages a thin smile. His eyes open a little more. It's as if life is returning to him in infinitesimal increments. The early days with my mother, when she seduced him with romantic torture, were probably the high points of his life.

"You fell for the dream, hook, line and sinker."

His face returns to its initial somber look. His eyes are sad, even a little mad. His head is tilted down. He clenches his teeth and jaw.

He tightens his grip on the armrests of the wheelchair. He breathes a little louder.

I'm already exhausted from this, and I haven't even gotten to the heavy part.

"Let's move on to the more important stuff."

He lets out a breath. He seems relieved to move on.

"So, after all these years, what did you think you were going to gain by killing my father and Timmy Wayne? Did you really believe Mom would return to you?"

He leans back a little, raises his head slightly and shakes it.

"I take that as a 'no.' Let me ask you this. How did you get my father and Timmy Wayne to lie down on the floor? I have a theory but would love to know the truth."

I wait, allowing the pause to fill the air around both of us. I so much want him to answer this. I look at him deeply, lean in a little, trying to connect in a way that provokes him to loosen his tongue. He has the answer and doesn't share it.

"I want to know what you did or said to make them so afraid they lay down. How long did it last? What did they say? Anything? What did you say? What was the damn plan? Did you take the Jeep? Did the dogs come, too? What did you do with the gun barrels?"

My voice rises at the end. He's not saying.

"I assume you dressed up as a police officer in full SWAT-like regalia to gain entry and get them to do what you wanted. Is that correct?"

I can see his mind unwinding time, reversing to the past. His mouth opens. Is he about to speak? He exhales and drops his eyes.

"On your drive to Conway from Utah to commit murder, what were you thinking? How did you occupy your time? What were your thoughts? I want to know."

He raises his head. He opens his mouth slightly and, holy shit, begins to speak. His voice is low and gravelly.

"I don't know. I was, uh, crazed. On meth. My mind was, um, numb. So long ago. Hard."

That handful of words exhausted him. I pick up the slack.

"After the murders, how did you feel? Anything? How did you think it would go? That you committed the perfect crime? Were you filled with joy, relief, power, victory like the mercenary solider you fancied yourself to be?"

I can tell that he's mining his mind for answers. I watch the search. Whatever he finds, he doesn't share.

"Tell me, did you think of me and Trey? Did you consider, even for a moment, how it might affect us? Did you give a shit?" My voice raises at the end. I shake inside.

Nothing.

"Or did you believe the murder would solve dysfunctional family problems?'"

He looks up quizzically. The question surprised him. He takes a breath that raises and drops his shoulders. For the first time, he looks normal, almost earnest. He nods slightly, not to me, to himself. He exhales again and speaks.

"I loved your mother." He bobs his head. "I would have done anything she asked me to do. I thought this is what she wanted." He straightens his back, as if gaining strength. "I thought if I did what I did, it would have made it better between us, that she'd come back to me." His voice trails off at the end and he looks away.

That is the answer I assumed he'd give, reflecting a delusional human being. I roll the dice on the next one.

"What did you tell my mom? Did you tell her you were going to kill my dad? Did she ask you to do it? Did her family ask you to do it? What did they say to you? Who helped you?"

He rocks back and forth in response. He stops moving and looks at me directly, a rare moment. He is taking those questions to the grave.

"Unfortunately for you, and the rest of us, you only made things worse. You and she were never going to be. Deep down, I believe you knew that, and it made you insane.

"What do you have to say for yourself? Help me understand. Is what I'm saying true?"

Nothing.

I am getting mad. I am feeling infuriated. I feel close to the edge of losing it.

"After you murdered my father and his friend, my mother wanted to rid herself of you like a flagrant STD. But you refused to go away. You couldn't let it go, you clingy bastard. You called my mother's family members, partly I think because you had no idea what else to do. You were fucking desperate. I also think you were skulking around to get information about what was happening with the murders. Feel free to correct me if I am wrong."

I don't give him a chance.

"My family felt sorry for you. They gave you updates. They apologized for my mom's behavior. But that wasn't good enough for you. You had to have her. You were obsessed and out of control. So, you formulated your next evil plan. Stop me any time I misfire here."

I fear I am losing him. But I can't stop.

"Kidnapping? Really? Fucking brilliant. I mean, what better way to make her love you than by kidnapping her. Did you totally lose your shit or what?

"Once you had her, what did you think you were going to do with her? Did you believe she was going to love you? You had a grave dug for her. Were you going to kill her if she didn't stay? Like, if you can't have her, no one can, or some crazy shit like that."

He seems off somewhere now. I try something to perk him up.

"Does it gnaw at you that had you not kidnapped my mother, had you limited your handiwork to the murders, the police might never have looked at you as a suspect? You could have gotten away with it. You know, as I think about it, and insane as it sounds, the kidnapping was a blessing in disguise. What do you think about that?"

He bobs up and down, and slightly smirks to himself in recognition. He has thought about that before, often, I'm guessing. He knows he did himself in. I enjoy the moment.

"I wish you'd have done me one last favor: shot yourself in the head. It would've been the best way to end this nightmare. When you kidnapped my mother, your life as a free man was over. You could have gone all the way by doing the deed. God knows, you had the means. It would have spared me an eleven-year struggle to get justice out of the courts, pissing people off, and making enemies by pushing hard for prosecution."

I am losing steam. My official visitation time is about over.

"When I came here today, I had nothing but hatred for you. I wanted you to burn in hell for eternity. I came with anger, grief, loss, deep hurt, and a yearning for revenge. I still feel much of that, but mostly now, I feel sorry for you, for how pitiful your life has become. I have no compassion for you. I hope you suffer guilt, despair, loss, pain, suffering and endless amounts of self-condemnation. I hope you wallow forever in misery. I'm done with you."

I lean way back and place my head on the back of the chair. I gaze at him, take a deep breath and release. It feels good. He looks back, nods a few times softly, and turns his wheelchair away from me. He wheels himself toward the door of the room, his back to me the whole time. He comes to a stop. Silence echoes between us. After about a minute, the guard opens the door to retrieve him. The guard glances at me and wheels Conte out of my presence. Conte never turns back, and I watch the door close behind him. He is gone forever.

EPILOGUE

Dear Daddy,

OH MY GOD DO I MISS YOU.

I have been through some shit since you left us. Each day I wonder what life would be like if you were still here, and how we would have evolved as father and daughter. We had our share of rough spots but we were making strides together. In my heart of hearts, I know we'd be on solid ground. It would be so good. I miss you badly.

I sometimes wonder what I'd be like without the grief and deep scars I carry under cover of silence. I don't dwell much. I'm not big on self-pity. But stopping those thoughts can be hard.

I wonder what you'd look like. I struggle to picture it, except I know your eyes, strikingly blue with characteristic glimmers of mischief, and your smile, slightly imperfect, although always perfect to me. You'd be wearing those glasses of yours. They soften you, making you look professorial. I've kept them. You wear them in my dreams. Our noses wrinkle the same now, despite the Botox. You'd still be athletic.

I have two children, a girl and boy, and a loving husband, Paul. It pains me you never met them. It gives me the deepest regret.

You'd adore and love my children and rejoice in your role of grandfather. Each is like you and me. They are opinionated, unbridled, and equipped with the acid tongue you gave me. I try to help them, I do, but it's hard, as I now appreciate how hard it was for you to deal with me. I long for your wisdom.

Samantha is a beautiful tomboy, quick-witted, and someone who doesn't take much from anyone. She is a "good" girl. She plays volleyball and is a way better child than I ever was, despite my parenting missteps.

I see you playing volleyball with her, challenging her each step of the way, and stubbornly believing you've still got it despite your age. I see you hanging with her at every serve, like you did with me when we'd run together. I'll never forget the time I managed to beat you! We were so competitive.

Oh, and my son, Ashton! You broke the mold when God created me but Ashton gives me a run for my money. He leaves me speechless each day. He can dish it out with the best of them but has yet to manage the process of handling the return. Time will help. He rises to challenges each day. He also tends to push the buttons of those around him. He is a great kid with so much energy to harness. Sound familiar? I often wonder how his life might be different with the devotion of your sage influence.

You and Paul would hit it off so well. He's a great man and you'd hold much respect for him. And I know he'd feel the same way toward you.

I picture us spending a lot of time in the winter in Park City, skiing often, even though—as you may remember—I hate being cold. I'd go because that is what we do as a family.

I see you taking us to the black diamond slopes. Samantha would refuse and Ashton would be up for it. I, of course, would keep a close on eye on Ashton and you, since you both have the kind of enthusiasm that increases the risk of injury.

While we skied, Samantha would go with Paul and stay on the greens. She is super comfortable saying "no" and doing what she wants.

I know you would dress up as Santa Claus at Christmas and run around outside in the snow and make sure the kids went to bed on time. I've retained our traditions and I'd rejoice in spending them with you.

Paul has five kids of his own, bringing our collective tribe to seven. You'd eat it up. There is, I assure you, never a dull moment. It is non-stop action. The kids would love and adore you like they do Mom.

I'd love to think we'd all assemble on holidays and enjoy time together. I see us renting a huge ski cabin for the entire family with Mom joining us. It would be beautiful. We would watch Christmas movies piled up together and you'd sing Bing Crosby songs. You would get Uncle Rusty or Uncle Matt to play Santa Claus for the kids, even though no one really believes in Santa. In your special way, you'd convince them that Santa won't pay them a visit unless they believed, just like you did for Trey, me, and our cousins.

I picture us going on a snowmobile adventure. We'd race and have our fair share of fun disasters that turned into warm memories. You'd be the ringleader, a role you cherished, and we'd get in line for the show. I wonder which kids would fall for your adventures and which would chicken out.

Oh, we'd go tubing, too!

You'd fill every day with something for everyone. The charity in your heart would be abundant and bless us all.

Yes, life would be so different with you here. It's still pretty much as good as it gets, please understand that. I love my husband and our children and have a rewarding life. I know you'd be content seeing how life has turned out for me. You'd be proud of me and I'd make you smile.

Imagining the impossible helps sometimes. It makes you part of my life, softens the hurt, and eases the pain of missing you. I know you'd feel nothing but love for me as I do for you.

Please continue to watch over us. Your spirit shall never die.

ACKNOWLEDGMENTS

I WANT TO THANK THE following for their help, guidance, and participation in the journey of writing this book.

Thank you, God, that I am still alive to write this. Thank you for your seasons and your timing. Thank you for allowing me to discover the "God" I believe in. Thank you for never leaving me or forsaking me.

Michael Coffino, my co-author, thank you for being my polished voice, diving into my life so willingly, and helping me create my beautiful truth. I remain grateful for your gentle feedback, willingness to listen to my occasional rants, and your professional guidance.

My Pastor, Randy Long: thank you for talking with me about my dad and taking time out of your life to relieve my pain. Thank you for never rejecting me. I am grateful for your open heart.

Lt. Jim Barrett, I am eternally grateful for your professional integrity, personal sense of honor, and diligent pursuit of justice. Amid all the chaos, investigative difficulties, and political gamesmanship, you never sold out: you stayed the course, consistently fighting for my daddy and Timmy Wayne, despite the naysayers. Thank you hearing me out and treating me with kindness and respect. Thank you from the depths of my soul.

Joan Shipley: despite the passage of time, and rush of your schedule, you were willing to answer my phone calls and provide information. Thank you. The sound of your voice reassured me that I was on the right track in this process. Women like you are a beacon of light for those of us in need of a kind and supportive word.

To the Jurors, thank you for seeing through the façade of Ralph Richard Conte and doing the right thing.

Carol Crews and your assistant Serena, thank you for the time you spent collecting and delivering judicial and investigative files about the murder of my father and Timmy Wayne. I know it was time consuming, but your efforts and willingness helped bring some closure to this nightmare. It is a relief to know more of the truth.

Thank you, Faulkner County 20th Judicial District, for showing me that the judicial system is a cruel teacher. You taught me many unforgettable lessons, to put it mildly.

Thank you, Ann Permenter, Cory Furness, Adam Waldron, FBI Special Agent Gerald Spurgers, FBI Special Affairs Officer Conner Hagen, Jack Lassister, and the Douglas County Sheriff's Office for providing time and information regarding events in this book. I am grateful for each of your contributions.

Thank you, Pamela McManus, transcriptionist extraordinaire, for your timely and unfailingly accurate interview transcriptions.

And, last but not the least, thank you, my loving husband, Paul, for being the gentleman you are and showing me love, kindness, and gentleness. Thank you for your uncommon patience and willingness to set and keep boundaries. Thank you for supporting me in my endeavors and loving my children unconditionally and treating them as your own. Thank you, most of all, for taking the vow.

ABOUT THE AUTHORS

ASHLEY ELLIOTT WAS BORN AND raised in the town of Conway, Arkansas and was by any measure proceeding on a traditional career path. After she turned twenty-five, and her wedding just months away, her life got turned inside out when her father was murdered and, a month later, her mother assaulted and kidnapped, entangling her for a decade with the criminal justice system and a relentless quest for justice.

The resulting trauma led to a diagnosis of PTSD and general anxiety, which she managed and overcame through therapy, family support, and the medium of writing.

The Demon in Disguise represents the culmination of a deep plunge into the center of her pain, and her painstaking exploration of her truth.

Ashley is an avid hiker, athlete, and bodybuilder, and has competed and won medals in various national and international athletic competitions, including the Spartan Worlds Championships and IPE Masters World Championships.

Ashley earned a B.S. from the University of Utah in Organizational Communication. She lives in Utah with her husband and children.

Michael J. Coffino

Before becoming a full-time writer and freelance editor, Michael Coffino had two parallel careers: one in the courtroom and the other in the gymnasium. He was a business litigation and trial attorney and legal writing instructor for four decades, and concurrently devoted twenty-five years as a basketball coach, primarily at the high school level.

He has written and co-authored nine books, including *Truth Is in the House*, his debut novel released in July 2021.

Michael grew up in the Bronx. He earned a B.S. in Education from the City University of New York, and a J.D. from the University of California, Berkeley, School of Law.

Michael plays guitar, holds a black belt in karate, is a workout junkie, plays pickleball, and hikes regularly in the hills and mountains of California and Colorado. He lives in Marin County, California and has two adult sons, both teachers and high school basketball coaches.

CPSIA information can be obtained
at www.ICGtesting.com
Printed in the USA
LVHW020400140821
694666LV00003B/11